THE HANDBOOK
OF
HANDGUNNING

Paul B. Weston

THE HANDBOOK
OF
HANDGUNNING

New Concepts in Pistol and Revolver Shooting

by

PAUL B. WESTON

Drawings by DON GRIFFITHS
Photographs by ERNEST TSUKUDA

CROWN PUBLISHERS, INC.   NEW YORK

Other Books by the Author

Target Shooting Today
Combat Shooting for Police
The Administration of Justice

CONTENTS

1

THE CONSTANT GRIP

LEARNING TO SHOOT A HANDGUN SHOULD START WITH YOUR FIRST contact with the weapon—picking it up. The best way to grip a handgun is just to shake hands with it. Fit the gun into the palm of your shooting hand just as the hand of a friend is grasped in greeting. Use a firm pressure, like a friendly handshake, on the gun. Do not use a "wet fish" or a "bonecrusher" pressure, but the grip normal to American adults.

A handgun may be a pistol or a revolver—a self-loading automatic, a modern double-action revolver, the classic six-shooter of frontier days, or one of the new magnum hunting handguns. The autopistol has a cartridge-feeding mechanism based on a magazine, while a revolver has a cylinder to hold its cartridges. When the handgun is an automatic, you must learn how to take out the magazine and lock the slide in an open position, how to make certain the chamber is empty, and how the safety latch functions. If the weapon is a modern revolver, you must be familiar with the simple operation of the cylinder latch, swinging out the cylinder, working the ejector rod, and making certain each chamber is empty. When the weapon is an old-timer, you need to know about the loading gate and how to rotate the cylinder to double-check for live ammunition.

Now, knowing your handgun is unloaded through personal examination, pick it up and shake hands with it. The gun should be so positioned by this hand-shaking procedure that a good portion of the backstrap (center of grip in the rear) is covered by the palm of your hand and the fleshy base of your thumb. The index (trigger) finger is free, resting outside of the trigger guard; the remaining fingers of the hand are wrapped snugly about the butt of the gun; and the thumb is placed along the side of the weapon at about the same level as the index finger.

SAFETY PRECAUTIONS

Basic rules for handgun safety are:

1. The only safe weapon is an empty gun, and a weapon is not to be considered as empty until it has been examined carefully and found to be empty, and the magazine removed and the chamber checked if an autopistol.

2. Never point a weapon, loaded or empty, in a direction where an accidental discharge may do harm.

3. When a weapon is in use, never place your finger within the trigger guard until you are ready to fire.

4. Never lay a loaded weapon down where someone may pick it up.

5. Before shooting at any practice session, check to see that the bore is free from dirt or any other obstruction.

The key to the most desirable grip for an individual marksman is in developing a way of grasping the weapon that can be used again and again, in exactly the same manner. Not only should the gun be grasped with the fingers in the same relationship every time it is fired, but it must also be gripped with a uniform and constant pressure.

Handgun Courtesy. Never hand a revolver to another person unless it is unloaded and the cylinder open. Autopistols must have their magazines out and the slide locked in its rearward or open position before transfer to another individual.

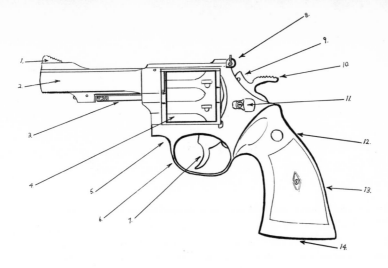

KNOW YOUR REVOLVER

1 Front sight.
2 Barrel; the muzzle is the front end of the barrel.
3 Ejector rod.
4 Cylinder; the chambers are the holes in the cylinder.
5 Frame.
6 Trigger guard.
7 Trigger.

8 Rear sight.
9 Hammer.
10 Hammer spur.
11 Cylinder latch.
12 Grip; the stocks are on either side of grip.
13 Backstrap.
14 Butt.

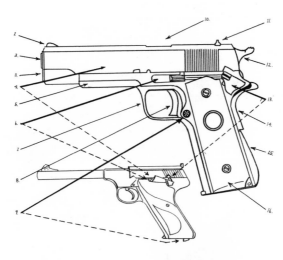

KNOW YOUR AUTOPISTOL

1 Front sight.
2 Barrel.
3 Barrel bushing.
4 Slide.
5 Receiver.
6 Slide stop (to lock slide to the rear in the open position).
7 Trigger guard.
8 Trigger.
9 Magazine release button.

10 Ejection port.
11 Rear sight.
12 Hammer.
13 Safety.
14 Grip safety.
15 Main spring housing.
16 Grip; stocks are on either side of grip, and the bottom of the grip is termed the "butt."

Note: Dotted arrows indicate similar parts on the .22 autopistol.

Turn your gun hand over slightly and look at your grip from the side. Is it unusually high or low on the grip? If the weapon is an automatic, the grip should be crowding the top rear portion of the pistol's frame where it fits into the base of the V of thumb–index finger. If a revolver, the grip should be crowding the space between the rear of the trigger guard and the front of the grip (usually filled in with a grip adapter or special stocks). The crowding keeps the grip from climbing after each shot as a result of recoil. Extend your arm to its fullest length without locking the elbow. Look **down**

The Handgun Grip. Below and opposite: The weapon is fitted into the center of the 'V' of the hand midway in the web between thumb and index finger, the thumb positioned high, the first joint of the index finger resting on the lower portion of the trigger, and the three remaining fingers wrapped firmly around the stock.

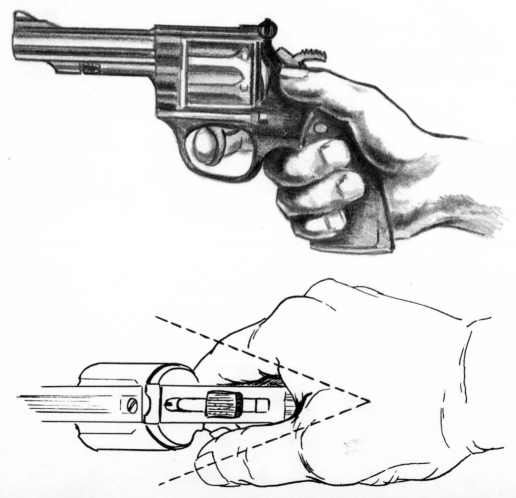

your arm. Is the barrel of the gun in natural extension of your arm? Do the thumb and index finger of your hand form a V, and is the center of the grip of the gun set somewhere in the middle of that V? If not, move the gun around in your hand until it is in this position, and try to attain a uniform handshake each time the gun is repositioned.

A good habit to develop is that of fitting the gun into the hand every time it is picked up for any reason. Grasp the metal portion of the handgun with the nonshooting hand just forward of the grip. Now fit your shooting hand to the butt of the gun, using your nonshooting hand to press the weapon snugly into your hand. Drop your nonshooting hand away from the gun. Put pressure into your handshake with the gun. The pressure points should be the front and the rear of the grip—do not dig in with the fingertips.

Uniformity

Try this grip pressure a few times. Novices cannot grip a
handgun very tightly; the tension sets up tremors in the
hand and arm that ruin any attempt to hold within a suitable
aiming area on a target. However, practice will increase the
firmness with which a gun can be grasped without setting
up tension tremors.

A handball or spring exerciser can be used to develop the musculature of the hand and arm. The important
thing to remember is that the pressure of the grip must be
uniform. In exercising to develop a firm grip, you should
concentrate on developing the muscles that hold the fleshy
base of the thumb firm against the rearward pressure of the
middle and ring fingers of the hand, and not cultivate the
muscles working the thumb or little finger.

Thumb pressure is not a digging-in but a resting of
the thumb upon the gun; little finger pressure is subordinated
to pressure with the middle and ring fingers. The pressure
with which a marksman's thumb rests upon a handgun or
the little finger rests upon the bottom of the grip depends
upon the firmness of the grip. A very firm grip is accompanied by very firm thumb or little finger pressure; a less
firm grip by less pressure. There must be a balancing in this
relationship of thumb and little finger to basic grip pressure.
Unbalanced pressure will flip a handgun away from its aiming area at the moment a shot is fired.

Before any shooting is attempted by the student-
reader, the gun must be grasped time and again until the
beginnings of a good grip are established. Later, as you
begin range firing, every opportunity should be taken to fit
the gun into the hand with a uniform grip until a feel is
developed. Uniformity, sought after and achieved, should
not be discarded lightly. Gross changes should not be made.
Stay with a good grip. If there is a need for change, confine

it to a minor change, and work at the new grip until it can be taken again and again, in the same manner.

Constancy

Constancy is akin to uniformity. The uniform manner in which the handgun is grasped each time it is picked up must be constant as it is aimed and fired.

There is a certain insidiousness about increasing grip pressure as a pistol or revolver is aimed and pressure is put upon the trigger. Possibly it is an attempt to hold the sights in better alignment—or just to reduce the shiver-and-shake of the gun—or to help in putting pressure on the trigger. It must be guarded against with continual watchfulness, for it ruins the skill potential of any shooter.

As a gun is aimed and fired, many shooters actually increase grip pressure to the point of muscle freezing, and

The Vise Grip. Top accuracy demands a constant viselike grip. The hand functions in a manner similar to the jaws of a vise: there is a fore-and-aft pressure on the grip that is tightened within the shooter's muscular limits and held firmly at that level—without increasing or decreasing grip pressure.

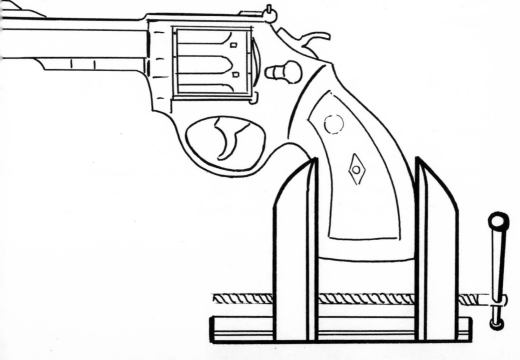

they are unable to put any pressure upon the trigger, squeezing the grip rather than the trigger. Often they force a spasmodic, jerking motion—pretty close to a convulsive muscle spasm—to actuate the trigger when they freeze on a grip, and this sudden motion makes them aware of **the exact moment** the weapon will fire. The sudden motion of trigger pressure may move the gun away from where it had been aimed; an awareness of when a handgun is going to fire leads to a pushing forward to meet the expected recoil.

Two other factors also require a constant grip in handgunning. First, sights cannot be held in careful alignment with each other when a gradually increasing pressure on the grip of a gun sets up tension tremors in the arm of a shooter which often double and triple the normal shiver-and-shake area in which a handgun is aimed. Second, there is a thing called "backslap" in the firing cycle of any handgun. It happens at the most important moment insofar as shooting accuracy is concerned—just as the weapon is fired. It is the continued rearward movement of the trigger **after** it has released the hammer. Gun manufacturers and gunsmiths cut down this travel, but some of it is necessary to provide clearance for the hammer to swing forward and fire the shot. A grip in which the pressure is increased during the aim-and-fire cycle has its top tension at the exact moment of trigger backslap—and the resultant movement of the gun **just as the hammer falls** effectively ruins accuracy.

The Trigger Finger

After you have worked at fitting the gun into your hand a few times, place your index finger on the trigger. There are several options: shoving it in so that the base of the finger rests against the side of the gun; bending it outward so that only the tip of the finger rests upon the trigger;

Testing the grip revolvers. The correct position for the back of a shooter's hand can be indexed with the hammer spur. Grip the gun naturally, reach for the hammer (to cock it) with the thumb, and note if the thumb is overreaching **(top)**, cannot quite reach the hammer spur **(center)**, or positions the hammer spur in the center of the fleshy pad of the first joint of the shooter's thumb **(bottom)**. Note **(top photo)** any attempt to cock the hammer with this grip would force a shooter to turn the gun to the side; in the center illustration, it would not be possible to cock the weapon with this low grip. The bottom picture indicates the manner in which a properly indexed grip allows the thumb to cock the hammer with a downward motion that does not move the weapon to the side and off the target as it is cocked.

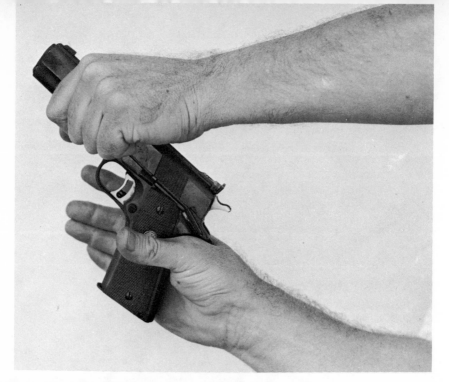

Testing the grip automatic pistols. In this two-hand test, the nonshooting hand grips the pistol and places it in the middle of the web of the shooting hand between thumb and index finger, with the rear of the grip being "indexed" by jamming the projecting grip safety extension at the top rear of the grip of these guns into the flesh of the web between these fingers. Then the three lower fingers are wrapped around the stock, and the thumb placed in position. The gun illustrated is a heavy-caliber military model automatic (.45 Gold Cup Colt), but the same indexing procedure can be used to test the grip on nonmilitary models of .22 caliber.

Trigger finger position. Opposite center: Using the tip of the finger only. This is about the minimum amount of finger to insert into the trigger guard. **Opposite bottom:** Using the entire first joint of the trigger finger. This is the maximum amount of finger to insert into the trigger guard.

or splitting the difference. It is a matter of preference, but again uniformity is essential. For shot-to-shot accuracy, try to place the same portion of the index finger on the trigger for each shot. The proper placing of the index finger on the trigger is part of the feel of a good grip.

There should also be a reaching-down of the index finger as it is placed upon the trigger of a revolver. These triggers are pinned in their upper portion and swivel to the rear. Therefore, the lower the index finger can be placed upon the trigger, the lighter the apparent pressure to swing it to the rear and fire the weapon. In shooting autopistols, the index finger should be centered on the trigger to ensure an even distribution of pressure as the trigger moves rearward in grooves cut into the receiver of the pistol. A marksman who complains of heavy trigger pressure or trigger "creep" may believe a weapon is defective when the apparent defect is the result of incorrect placement of the index finger on the trigger of the handgun.

Cocking the Revolver

One of the advantages of shooting autopistols, or shooting revolvers double-action, is that the weapon does not have to be cocked manually. The autopistol is returned to firing position again by the effect of recoil, and the revolver is fired in double action by trigger pressure without any major change in the grip. However, in firing a revolver single-action, the thumb must be taken from its resting place and utilized in cocking the hammer, and then returned to the same spot with the same pressure. All too often this motion of cocking a revolver degenerates into a juggling session in which the basic grip is relaxed and frequently lost entirely. The middle and ring fingers of the hand retain grip pressure, the fleshy ball of the thumb is placed upon the hammer spur with a downward and rearward pressure, a bending of the thumb, until the hammer is cocked, and then the thumb is promptly returned to its resting place. This must be developed, through practice, into a smooth motion in which the hammer is cocked by thumb movement without bending the elbow or twisting the muzzle of the weapon a great deal off target, and this cocking motion becomes an automatic reflex after firing a shot.

A grip high on a revolver is fine in double-action shooting, but cramps the thumb when cocking the hammer in single-action firing. The vertical grip adjustment can be tested by taking a grip and reaching for the uncocked hammer to make certain the thumb is positioned so that it can be bent without difficulty.

Grip Hazards

There are a half-dozen common faults that must be guarded against **every time** a handgun is fired. As a shooter fits a gun into his hand, and as he aims and fires it, there is a subliminal checking of these grip hazards. Actually, it is nothing more nor less than a rapid mental review of some of

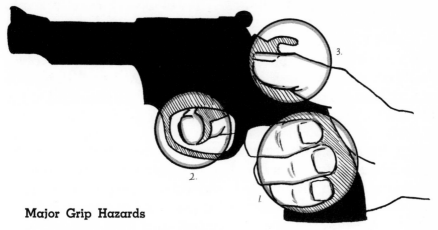

Major Grip Hazards

1. Fingertips digging into stock;
2. Faulty trigger finger placement; and
3. Thumb not returned to the same position after each shot, or digging in with excessive pressure.

the pitfalls associated with gripping a handgun. It is impossible to say which of the common faults is most likely to be encountered. Some shooters seem to favor certain poor habits; others believe in variety.

The six most common grip hazards are:

1. Fingertips digging into the stock—a tension-builder. Watch for the telltale white half-moons under the fingernails.
2. Faulty trigger finger placement—index finger incorrectly placed on trigger, or finger moved to different positions on the trigger from shot to shot.
3. Thumb problems—the thumb not placed in the same position of rest for each shot, or digging in with excessive pressure.
4. "Pinkie muscle"—too much pressure at the bottom of the grip.
5. Movement—grip not cramped against weapon to

prevent movement when shooting and in rapid fire.

6. Gun not centering in V of grip—there is some variation possible in centering the gun, and it is often impossible for individuals with small hands to center a gun accurately, but a grip too far to one side or the other is undesirable.

The basic characteristics of a good grip are uniformity and an unchanging pressure against a background of the hazards that trap the unwary shooter. Practice taking a uniform grip, extending the arm up and forward to its full length, and holding the handgun with a grip pressure that neither diminishes or increases: a constant grip.

2

THE BASIC POSITION

A STABLE SHOOTING POSITION, PLUS A CONSTANT GRIP, PROVIDES THE necessary base or foundation for aiming and firing a handgun with accuracy. In combat shooting or hunting with a handgun, increased stability may be obtained by resting the gun hand on a barricade, the knees, or some other support. The classic pistol-shooting position for target practice requires the marksman to stand without support of any kind. The stability of any shooting position is enhanced by avoiding muscular tension. Even when the pistol or revolver is rested against a support, muscular tightness can ruin the effectiveness of any shooter. A tightened muscular system spells out tensions that pull a handgun **away** from its target at the moment of firing. Relax, but do not collapse. A stable position is keyed to controlled relaxation. Surprisingly, the eyes are the basis for a relaxed position in either target shooting or in combat defense. The body responds to an initial visual clue: the line of sight.

The Line of Sight

The line of sight is a simple but important concept in handgunning. It is simply a matter of looking at an area at which you are going to aim the gun, and bringing the gun up into this line of sight as the arm is extended to its full length. The body's muscular system is not tensed in merely looking at an aiming area, and if care is exercised in bringing a handgun up into the line of sight, the shooter's body can remain relaxed. A shooter who looks and then points his weapon gains a position of naturalness using only those

Raise Pistol. A position of rest before shooting, between shots, and after firing. Pistol range discipline demands this position except when the weapon is being fired, loaded, or unloaded. The muzzle of the gun is **down range,** the grip relaxed with the trigger finger **outside** of the trigger guard; and the elbow rests easily against the body.

muscles necessary to bring the gun up into aiming position and hold it there.

The best stance from which to establish a line of sight is the "Raise Pistol" position. This is a position of rest, the gun is fitted into the shooter's hand, the index finger is outside the trigger guard, the barrel axis is at a 45-degree angle toward the target, and the elbow rests against the body. This puts the muzzle of the gun down range, about six to eight inches ahead of the shoulder and **below** the line of sight. In this position, the visual concentration is directed toward the aiming area, and the pistol or revolver is moved up and forward until the sights settle in front of the eyes

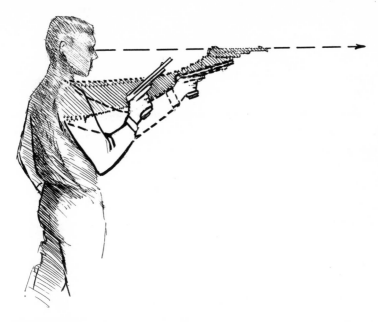

Body Position and Line of Sight. The shooter looks at his target after taking his position, and from **Raise Pistol** brings his handgun up and into his line of sight.

directly on the line of sight. When this up-and-forward movement is executed properly (without any unnecessary movement of the gun) the shooter learns to move into an aiming position simply by pointing the gun where he is looking.

Practice picking up a line of sight and bringing the handgun up to intercept the line. Fit your handgun into your hand with a uniform and constant grip. Take the "Raise Pistol" position. Remember, it is a position of rest. Relax. Pick an aiming area. Look at it. Bring the gun up and forward until the shooting arm is fully extended without forcing the elbow to lock, and the sights settle into the established line of sight. Be careful not to move your head down to meet the gun. Try it from the sitting position. Standing. Kneeling. It is the same procedure from any position. It would be the same movement if the weapon was drawn from a holster.

The Basic Shooting Position

The ideal shooting position is a comfortable stance adapted to the general physical structure of individual shooters. Comfort and controlled relaxation, like love and marriage, go together. A twisted neck that tenses muscles in the face and chest areas is not comfortable, and a locked-knee position tight with tension will tire a marksman after even a short session. In fact, tension can become so great in some cases that actual physical pain can be detected in some part of the body.

A basic three-step footwork is helpful in securing a comfortable position. The shooter faces the target squarely, with feet together; turns left (right-handed shooters) about a quarter face or 45 degrees; and then spreads his feet about 16 to 18 inches apart. Try this movement several times. It is

Position Footwork. The three-step procedure for achieving the same position time after time is standardized with practice. Begin by facing the target with both feet together, gun at **Raise Pistol;** take a quarter face to the left (right-hand shooters), about 45°; spread the feet about shoulder width and extend the shooting arm toward the target. Shooters may vary this position slightly, but it is important that they develop this methodology of taking a shooting position as top accuracy demands shooting from the same position every time the gun is fired.

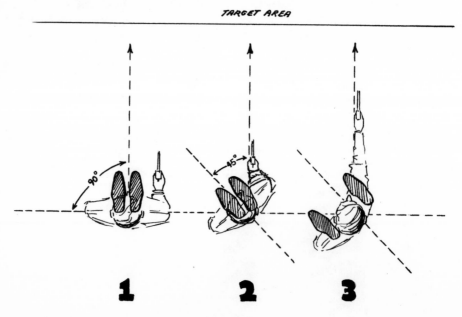

TARGET AREA

1   **2**   **3**

The Target Shooting Position. Controlled relaxation: holding the handgun on target without muscular tension provides a stable shooting platform for sighting, aiming, and firing. The author is firing his Colt .45 Gold Cup National Match on the campus pistol range at Sacramento State College, Sacramento, California.

helpful for shot-to-shot accuracy to drop into the same position every time the handgun is fired, and this three-step
method provides a routine for putting the feet in the same
relationship to the shooting position each time the position is
assumed. Some shooters face the target more squarely, and
back tension may develop in this stance. Others who face
away from the target more than 45 degrees not only develop
body tension but often sway slightly from side to side. Tension will occur in the legs when the feet are placed too close
together, and some body sway may be present. A spread-
eagle position with the feet wide apart may be structurally
sound as a base for shooting, but develops massive body
tensions—unless special exercises have prepared a shooter
for this position.

Basic tensions built up in the legs, when they are not
in a spread-eagle position, usually result from tightly locked
knees. This does not mean that the handgun should be fired
from a bent knee position, but it does mean that tightness in
the knee area will tense the entire lower body. Since this is
the foundation area, it is easy to see how a little tension at
the bottom can be magnified at the top—the end of the arm.
Leg tension adds at least 10 percent to a shiver-and-shake
motion when aiming.

A good procedure for discovering tension in the knee
area is to flex the knees slowly several times just before
extending the arm into the aiming position. This is a barely
perceptible movement, just a loosening-up exercise that is
very helpful in developing a good foundation.

The head, waist, shoulders, and arms are also vital
body areas to be considered in taking a comfortable position.

When the basic aiming procedure is keyed to pointing the gun along a line of sight, the head will be held
without neck tension. Many experienced shooters fail to
realize just how much tension can be developed in the entire
upper body by dropping the head down or twisting it to one
side. Many have found their normal shiver-and-shake aiming

Neck Tension. Left: Shooter's head is erect and he brings the gun up to his line of sight. Correct. **Right:** Shooter has bent his head down to meet his aimed weapon, creating tension in the neck area. Incorrect.

Neck Tension. Author demonstrates a common fault: head bent forward, tightening up neck muscles and forcing shooter to sight through his eyelashes. When head is held erect note improvement in visual plane and lack of tension in face and neck muscles.

The Nonshooting Arm. Left—Incorrect: Arm is used as a prop and shooter usually develops waist tension because of tendency to lean back. **Center—Incorrect:** Free-swinging arm transmits movement to entire body and ruins sighting and aiming. **Right—Correct:** Hand in left trousers pocket pins down nonshooting arm in a relaxed position.

area to be reduced as much as 20 percent when they corrected a basically poor head position and relieved tension in the neck area.

Leaning back from the waist is almost a classic fault. It starts with beginners who have difficulty in holding a heavy handgun in the aiming position. A small amount of leaning does not matter, but some shooters lean back a little more as each shot is fired, with increasing body tension building up until the last shot is fired from a bowed position. Others appear to lean back to a greater degree with each range session until their bowed position creates so much tension as to remind them to straighten up. The best safeguard against becoming a leaner is to displace the weight of the body slightly **forward,** toward the balls of the feet, every time the three-step footwork is performed in taking the correct basic position. It is a case of facing the target, turning left, spreading the legs, and leaning **slightly** forward on the balls of the feet.

The shooting arm's shoulder should not be hunched

up into a knot of muscular tension. As the shooting arm is extended into the line of sight, there is a natural flexing of the arm up and forward. The elbow is neither bent nor locked —the arm is simply extended to its full length without strain. Most shooters can easily observe a bent or locked elbow, but a great many of them cannot tell when they are raising the shoulder unnaturally as the arm is extended into the aiming position. Take position several times. Extend the arm up and forward **without raising the shoulder.** Of course, you can shoot well with a hunched-up shoulder, but I have changed several top marksmen on police and service pistol teams over to a natural-shoulder position and their scores have improved. Tension in the shoulder area probably increases shiver-and-shake when aiming by at least 10 percent.

The free arm of a shooter is not a problem when it is shoved without tension into his side pants pocket. Rested on the hip, or placed in a hip pocket, it can cause body tension from a tendency to lean back against its support. When permitted to hang loosely at the side, this arm will sway slightly and threaten the stability of the entire body position.

Combat Positions

Combat positions for aimed fire range from the "barricade" position through sitting and kneeling to the prone position, and provide both support for the gun and target reduction for the shooter. However, all combat positions for aiming and firing require the extended arm position for both stability and sight definition. Bending the shooting arm's elbow in these positions creates unexpected body tensions, and the shortened distance between the shooter's eyes and the gun's sights makes it difficult to align the sights and aim the handgun with the necessary care.

The barricade position is a two-hand position in

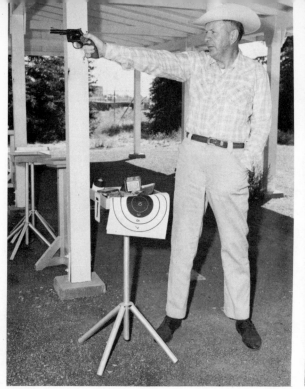

Two-hand combat or hunting position. The author demonstrates the difference between the standard target position and the two-hand combat or hunting position. Note that the basic grip on the handgun does not change. The left foot is brought forward, the right hand grasps the base of the shooting hand, and the gun is moved over toward the center of the shooter's body. This is an excellent position for steadiness and for rapid fire. The triangular support of both arms cuts down on the swing-and-sway motion and permits better control in getting the gun back on target for following shots in rapid fire. Police often use this position, resting both arms on a car's top or other support. It is also the top "structure" of the two-hand combat kneeling position and the standard combat sitting position.

which the base of the nonshooting hand is rested against the barricade. This may be a fencelike structure on the pistol range, but in combat it is usually any wall or other support that happens to be available. The shooter stands behind the barricade—attempting to conceal as much of his body as possible—and leans against it for greater relaxation and to lessen his normal shiver-and-shake aiming area.

In both the sitting and the kneeling position both hands hold the gun, and the body structure of the shooter is the basic support. These positions lessen the target area by about 50 percent. The California sitting position sacrifices two-hand support in order to secure greater relaxation by

CALIFORNIA POLICE TRAINING

Above: Stockton police officers firing prone at the 60-yard stage of the practical pistol course of fire. This is a position of high target reduction and stability.

Right: Highway Patrol Academy instructors John Mahe **(left)** and John Pedri demonstrate the "California Sitting Position." Note the trusslike support in the position of the leg under the gun arm's wrist.

COMBAT SHOOTING POSITION—TWO-HAND KNEELING

The most popular of the combat shooting positions. The Massachusetts State Police developed this position. It can be assumed with speed, it offers target reduction, and it is supported by the shooter's body structure. Note two-hand grip and fully extended arms; shots can be fired very rapidly and accurately from this position.

using the nonshooting hand to brace the upper body of the shooter in a relaxed position of great steadiness—and comfort. The Massachusetts two-hand kneeling position, in which the back is held straight and no support is provided for the clasped hands of the shooter, sacrifices support for a position into which a shooter can drop rapidly, with some target reduction and real surprise in the changed aspect of the target viewed by an opponent. This is a position in which shots can be rocked off with amazing rapidity and accuracy.

The prone position offers the greatest support and target reduction, but it is also the most difficult in which to relax because the position forces the head to bend back sharply in order to aim the gun and creates terrific body tensions unless considerable practice loosens up the neck muscles.

Breath Adjustment

Hold your breath without strain when shooting—do not go into near-strangulation. Adjustment of breathing for handgunning must be accomplished on the subconscious level when shooting or it will intrude and break up the shooter's capability for concentrating on sight alignment and trigger let-off. There must be some holding of the breath to steady the arm in the aiming position, but it must be done smoothly and without building up thoracic tension.

The thoracic area is that portion of the upper body between the neck and the abdomen, and supported by the ribs. It is an area of movement and therefore muscular structure. Almost centered in this area is the diaphragm, the partition within the body separating the chest and the abdominal cavities. Heavy breathing, at both inspiration and expiration, involves movements of both the diaphragm and the

rib cage. Breathing when at rest involves only slight movements, and the diaphragmatic tension is relaxed at expiration.

Try this a few times: Take a couple of heavy or deep
breaths, and a few light or shallow breaths. Note the considerable tension at inspiration during heavy breathing—
how the entire thoracic area seems tight when the lungs are
bursting-full of air. Now note the completely opposite picture,
the fine feeling of relaxation at expiration during shallow
breathing. Now exhale only about half of the air taken in
during one of the shallow breaths and note the relaxed feeling in the entire chest and abdominal area—and also note
that the diaphragm is relaxed or collapsed. This is the breathing adjustment most helpful to good shooting.

A studied attempt at breath adjustment must be
made when beginning to shoot a pistol or revolver. It is somewhat like learning proper breathing for swimming the crawl
stroke. It must be timed to coincide with the aiming-and-firing
cycle, just as in swimming it must be timed with the swimming stroke. However, in either case, once learned it is
nothing more than a conditioned reflex, something that is
done without conscious thinking.

Try a few deep breaths for relaxation generally, and
a few shallow breaths. Now expel only about 50 percent of
the air in the lungs, and hold the remaining air without
diaphragmatic tension—just close off the breath in the throat
by stopping the expiration of air. Without tension, this air
can be held comfortably—and that is what is meant by
correct breath adjustment. Try it again and again. Now, fit
the gun into your hand, take a grip pressure that will be
constant—unchanging. Slip into the basic shooting position,
and come to "Raise Pistol." Establish a line of sight with head
erect and body without tension, take a few shallow breaths,
shut off one at half capacity, and time it with the extension
of the gun arm into the line of sight and aiming position.
Hold it—without tensing the chest or belly area (diaphragm)

—as the arm is held at shoulder level. When it becomes un-
comfortable, expel the air and bring the arm back to "Raise
Pistol." Try this quite a few times, until it can be done without
really thinking about it.

Common Faults

Controlled relaxation in shooting requires the traditional
eternal vigilance. Shooters must check themselves time and
time again, and make certain they have not drifted into
some of the more common faults. True, a minor fault is
difficult to determine solely on the basis of comfort. Probably
the condition which should alert a shooter to body tension is
an increase in the shiver-and-shake area when aiming. It is
a warning that his foundation is shaky.

A check list generally includes the areas of the body
concerned with the most common faults. These are:

1. The head
2. Shooting-arm elbow
3. Hunched-up shoulder
4. Free arm
5. Waist area
6. Legs and knees
7. Thoracic area.

Remember, the basic shooting position begins with
a response to the visual clue of looking at an aiming area
and is safeguarded against tension by constant vigilance
and a repetition of a standard procedure of moving into
position. A shooter must "groove" his shooting position; it
must be taken naturally each time; and it must be a position
of controlled relaxation providing a stable foundation for
shooting.

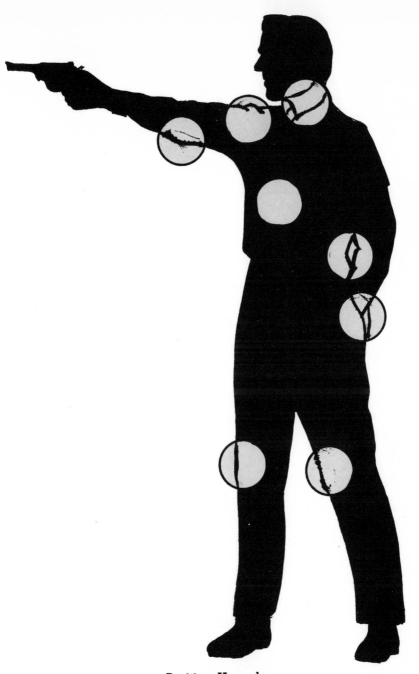

Position Hazards

Elbow bent or locked in place.

Shoulder tightened or hunched.

Tension in neck area; head bent forward or to one side.

Chest tension due to improper breath control.

Waist tension; leaning back from the waist.

Left hand (right-hand shooters) jammed into pocket; or swinging
   at side.

Tension in knee areas.

3

SIGHTING

SIGHT ALIGNMENT IN HANDGUNNING IS AN APPARENTLY SIMPLE THING that most shooters foul up time and time again, and usually solely as a result of failing to **concentrate continually** during the aiming-and-firing cycle **upon the two sights in relation to each other.**

It seems almost ridiculous to stress the need for sight alignment. Sights were placed on guns as reference points by which to aim them. That shooters would carelessly ignore or subordinate such an elementary need in shooting is unbelievable. Words of caution usually alert any individual to some level of watchfulness. "Look out below" is usually a prelude to a person's looking up. "Watch your step" is generally followed by a downward focusing of the eyes. And a plain "Look out!" usually alerts all the senses of any person. This is why it is so very strange that words of caution do not alert shooters to watch their sights with the vigilance necessary for good shooting.

The importance of sight alignment, the two sights in relationship to each other, is easy to demonstrate. Take a short pencil, hold one end and move the other end slightly. Note the distance laterally. Take a longer pencil and do the same thing, notice how the same lateral movement is increased when a longer pencil is moved. Do the same thing with two of your fingers. Make a V. At the base, the fingers are still close together, but they are far apart at their tips. Now, when an error is made in sight alignment when aiming a handgun with a 6-inch sight radius (distance between front and rear sights), what is the error when extended to 75 feet? Work it out along the lines indicated by the V of your fingers. The error in sight alignment is going to be magnified in relationship to the distance to the target—a terrific amount. Sight alignment errors form an angle of error that increases in mathematical progression along the path of the bullet.

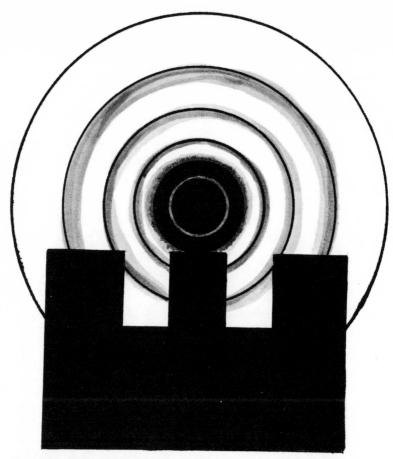

Looking at the Sights. This is the correct sight picture. The
sights are clear and sharp and bright; the target is indistinct,
fuzzy, and blurred.

Intrasight Relationships

In the aiming position, because of their short sight radius,
the sights of a handgun are seen in a close relationship:
the front sight seems to be sitting in the rear sight notch.
And it is this togetherness that must be developed to achieve
top accuracy with a handgun.

There are four basic reference points in the intrasight
relationship in handgunning. These are:

1. The rear sight notch
2. The body of the front sight
3. The top of the front sight

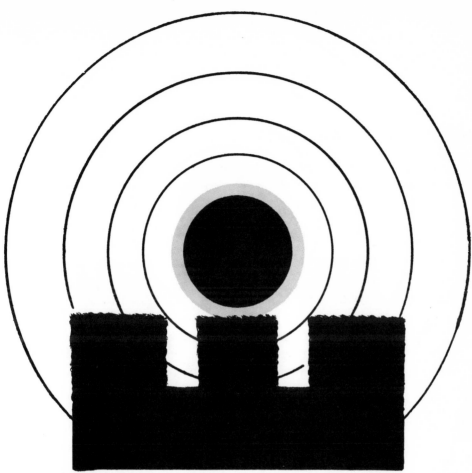

Sighting Hazard. This is an incorrect sight picture. The shooter is concentrating visually upon the target and downgrading the two major reference points for accuracy in handgunning: the front and rear sights in relation to each other. The warning of this hazard is a blurring of the sights and a sharp image of the target.

4. The top of either side of the rear sight immediately adjacent to the rear sight notch.

However, there is also a fifth relationship inherent in the first two, and this is the **line of white** on either side of the front sight when it is placed in the rear sight notch during the aiming-and-firing stage. It is now known as a means for the effective correlation of the four basic intrasight relationships.

Briefly, correct sight alignment is summed up as follows: Line up the two sights with each other by placing the body of the front sight squarely in the middle of the rear sight notch with the top of the front sight on a level with the top of the rear sight. The line of white on either side of the body of the front sight is exactly the same on both sides when the front sight is aligned correctly, and it is continual watchfulness and supervision over the line-of-white dimensions on either side of the front sight that aids a shooter in holding the front sight squarely in the middle of the rear sight notch and serves to guide the top of the front sight to a level with either side of the rear sight notch.

The dimensions of these reference points are important. Generally, it is easier to align a wide (about ⅛-inch) front sight in a generous notch in a rear sight, and it can be done more rapidly. The fat lines of white on either side act as a ready reference. On the other hand, thin lines of white, or a narrow front sight, or both, are difficult to hold in focus and often blur into a fuzzy sight picture in which it is difficult or impossible to align the two sights. Individual shooters must find the combination best suited to their own eye power.

As guidelines for new shooters it will be well to remember that a wide front sight and a generous rear sight notch can be aligned with accuracy and speed—and a flat-top rear sight makes it easier to keep the tops of the two sights in correct alignment.

The depth of the notch in the rear sight is of some importance—within reasonable limits. A fairly deep notch makes the lines of white in the sight picture somewhat easier to line up, but when it is cut too deep it draws the eyes away from the tops of the two sights and makes it more difficult to hold the horizontal alignment.

Focus

The eyes of the shooter should be focused directly upon the handgun sights. The normal shooting distance for pistols and revolvers is never so great that any need exists for a shuttling back and forth of visual concentration between the sights and the target. In handgunning, the sights are the object of visual concentration (in their togetherness), and the shooter sees the target in his secondary vision—definitely out of focus. This is the reason shooters around the world are told by pistol instructors: "You must see the sights clearly, but it is **not** necessary that your aiming area upon the target be equally clear."

No one can actually focus his eyes on an object an arm's length away and an object at 25 yards distant at the same time. What is usually misconstrued as this double focusing is in reality a rapid shuttling of the eyes back and forth. Some experienced shooters do this, many of them without being aware of it, and it does not ruin accuracy if it does not end up by changing the focus of the eyes to either the target alone or the target and the front sight.

It is this almost-normal, and therefore quite common tendency to look **through** the sights at the target, or **through** the rear sight notch at the front sight and the target, that created the instructional theme: "Look **at** the sights, not **through** 'em."

When a shooter looks through the sights, the front sight is outlined clearly against the target, but the rear sight and its notch are blurred and out of focus—and since the basic reference points in sight alignment are the **two** sights, little accuracy is possible. A warning that the viewing is not being concentrated on the two sights occurs when a shooter notices that the lines of white are indistinct, fuzzy, and hairy. This is termed "losing the rear sight."

It was the great need for focusing upon the sights, rather than on the target, that led to the adoption by most coaches of the area aiming concept: aiming in an "area" on the target, rather than at an aiming "point." The aiming point acts as an attractive nuisance and draws the eyes of a shooter into looking away from the sights and at the target. Of course, the fact that no one can hold a gun absolutely steady at arm's length was the major factor in developing the concept of area aiming, but the problem of focusing the eyes correctly has been partially solved by this idea of **not attempting to be too precise as to just where the two aligned sights are aimed upon the target.**

Binocular Vision and the Master Eye

The stronger of a person's eyes is termed the master eye. It is the eye that should be placed directly behind the gun when aiming. If you do not know which is the master eye, a simple test will identify it. Hold a pencil at arm's length and cover some object with it, using both eyes. Now close one eye. If the pencil does **not** "move" away from the covered object, then your master eye is the one you have open. If it moves away, try closing the other eye.

Two-eyes-open sighting is best for combat shooting and less tiring when shooting over a long period. It is not difficult to develop the ability to shoot with both eyes open. This binocular vision aids in aligning the sights as everything is less "flat" and has dimensions in depth. Shoot if you wish with one eye closed, making certain it is not your master eye, but every now and then—after you have lined up the sights with each other—slowly open the closed eye. If the sights move or get out of focus, close the eye quickly, realign the sights, and repeat the process. Do this exercise an increasing number of times when sighting the gun, and in a short time you will achieve binocular vision—and enjoy shooting with both eyes open.

Vision is better when the position of the head is such that the eyes are not too far off center when aiming. The recommended basic shooting position almost guarantees this point by stressing the importance of keeping the head erect and steady, and the neck not twisted in any way. This is another reason to caution against dropping the head, as the eyes are not only off center, but also look out through the eyelashes in aligning the sights. A twisted neck sometimes brings the eyes so far off center that normal vision cannot be achieved even with both eyes open.

Just in case you cannot achieve binocular vision conveniently, go ahead and shoot with your master eye open, but do not screw your facial and neck muscles into a knot just to keep one eye closed. An otherwise stable and tension-free position can be ruined by unnecessary tension in holding an eyelid shut.

The Grip as a Factor in Sighting

A constant grip helps to hold the sights in alignment. When the muscles of the hand hold the handgun in a constant grip, the unchanging pressure on the grip aids in holding the sights in alignment with each other and the "set" of this type of grip keeps the wrist tightened up the necessary amount for a firmness in this area that will also prevent the sights from shaking about in relation to each other. There will be a shiver-and-shake motion at the end of your arm, but it must be controlled so that the whole arm and gun swing about **together**, and not separately and in different directions.

All shooters must understand why a differing pressure on the handgun's grip from shot to shot, or an increasing pressure as the trigger is pressed, will interfere with holding the sights in alignment with each other. This is also true of the need of a constant (and firm) grip to hold the wrist as an unmoving joint between the hand and arm. Try it. It is self-instructing. Pick up the empty gun (check it), point it in a safe direction (check that, too), and line up the sights with each other. Get a good sight picture. Now squeeze harder on the grip—and watch the sights move out of alignment. Do it again. This time tighten the grip pressure somewhere—possibly dig in with the thumb or little finger—and again sight

the gun. Now, note the sights moving about in their alignment. Loosen up the grip so the wrist of the shooting arm
feels loose, and **try** to hold the two sights in alignment—it is
difficult.

Sighting Is Pointing

Another highly instructive trial-and-error procedure relates
to the hazard of holding the sights in alignment with a
slight pressure to either right or left upon the trigger with
the index finger. This will ruin accuracy as it flips the gun
in a reaction to this pressure during the trigger backslap
period (just as the hammer falls and just before the weapon
fires), a really vital moment for accuracy. Line up the sights
a few times. Let them drift out of alignment slightly, then
bring them back with a pressure of the index finger to one
side or the other on the trigger. Note that it can be done, but
now quickly release the side pressure on the trigger as you
watch the sight alignment. You will see the sights flip back
into misalignment—and this is exactly what happens when
a gun is fired. It is ruinous. **Avoid side pressure on the trigger
when aligning the sights.**
     Sights cannot be held in alignment with a changing
grip pressure or a loose wrist. If there is any shaking in the
relationship of the sights to each other it is near-disaster for
the shooter. Side pressure on the trigger to .hold sights in
alignment is not easily detected and can ruin accuracy as
the handgun bounces away from where it had been aimed
because of the release of this pressure at the moment of
firing. A normal shiver-and-shake of the entire arm will not
hurt accuracy because it is controllable, but movement
within the alignment is ruinous. The gun points where it is
apparently aimed only when a constant grip is joined with
a careful alignment of the sights with each other.

4

AREA AIMING

AREA AIMING IS BASED ON THE BELIEF THAT IT IS DIFFICULT TO HOLD a handgun as "steady as a rock," and holding on an aiming point leads to an attempt to make the gun go off when the aligned sights are hanging precisely on this aiming point. The resultant awareness that the handgun is about to fire leads to poor habits such as jerking (sudden trigger pressure), or flinching and heeling (lunging forward to meet the pushing-back of recoil). Area aiming recognizes and accepts the fact that any marksman naturally wavers (shivers and shakes, in fact) in aiming a pistol or revolver, and that this wavering motion itself does not cause poor scores, but poor scores will occur when **sudden** trigger-finger motion habits develop from attempts to aim the handgun at a point on the target despite this wavering.

The beginning concept of area aiming was based on the idea that sudden trigger pressure or flinching would move the bullet's point of impact away from where it had been aimed. This "away" theory has been proved. Any sudden trigger pressure or lunging forward will move the gun **away** from wherever it had been aimed, and this sudden trigger pressure and possible flinching, or both, move the gun much farther away from this aiming point than any natural sway.

Sure, as a shooter gains experience he can be really precise in his "holding" and fire six to eight shots out of each string of ten with remarkable accuracy by making the gun go off just when it is "hanging" on an aiming point. Even sudden trigger pressures can be put on smoothly—most of the time. Even the lunging forward characteristic of flinching can be controlled—most of the time. Unfortunately for the peace of mind of these shooters, shots are scored in groups of ten, with accuracy being judged by the size of the group. This means that "most-of-the-time" accuracy is not good

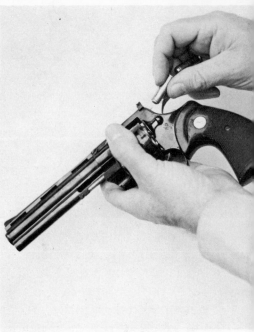

The loading position. The revolver is held in the left hand, muzzle down range, thumb and middle finger grasping the cylinder. As the cartridges are inserted into each chamber, the thumb and middle finger grasping the cylinder rotate it, and when the standard loading of five cartridges for target shooting is completed, close it with the empty chamber on top—in a position to move out of the way when the cylinder revolves as the first shot is fired.

The unloading position. The revolver rests in the palm of the left hand (right-handed shooters), muzzle down the range. The left thumb actuates the ejector rod and pushes out the empty cartridge cases. The right hand is used to catch the empty shells.

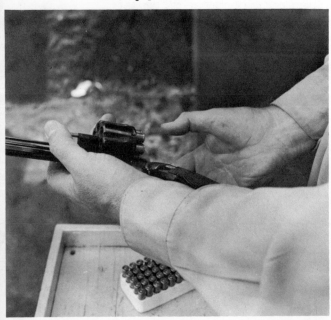
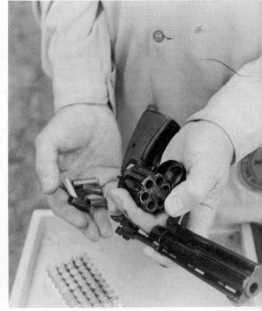

The stagger or "Swiss" * loading for viewing trigger motion. During loading of a revolver both empty cartridge cases and live cartridges are arranged alternately or at random, with two or three live rounds in each loading of the cylinder. A shooting partner or coach loads the weapon in this fashion, closes the cylinder, and hands the gun to the shooter. The shooter does not know whether or not the revolver will fire when he presses the trigger, but when the hammer falls on a **fired cartridge** the shooter can observe **any movement** of the gun at this vital moment. In the Sacramento State College coach-and-student instructional system, the coach not only stagger-loads the handgun but also serves as an observer and commentator.

This system can be adapted to automatic pistols by the use of "dummy" cartridges. These are usually fired cartridge cases in which bullets are reinserted to allow functioning in the feeding mechanism, and they generally have holes drilled in the side of the cartridge for identification purposes.

enough. This is also true of hunting and self-defense shooting: shot-after-shot accuracy is essential. It is not good enough to shoot very well 60 to 70 percent of the time—misses and near-misses count.

The desire of all shooters to excel, to shoot better than their friends and associates or to improve upon previous scores fired, handicaps total acceptance of the concept of

---

* Swiss loading is a term often used, and though no one has been able to trace its origin, it is usually assumed that the loading of empty cartridge cases makes holes in the loading of a revolver's cylinder similar to those in Swiss cheese.

area aiming. Shooters always try to improve, but in hand-gunning improvement must skirt known hazards to good shooting.

The sudden trigger-finger motion necessary to make a handgun fire will not move the point of impact a great distance away from where the weapon had been aimed, if it is made smoothly, but it is the awareness that the gun is about to fire that develops a massive flinching that will move the point of impact a foot or more.

It is the autonomic nervous system that defeats point-aim shooting. This is the body's system for warding off attacks or informing us when to flee, or both. It governs actions that are more or less automatic, and despite attempts at controlling the tendency to flinch, there is always the likelihood of an involuntary movement forward when the mind of the shooter is aware the gun is about to go off. The perception is that there is going to be a noise and something of a blow—and the autonomic nervous system's reaction is more or less uncontrollable.

The Shiver-and-Shake Area

Novice shooters just have to accept the fact that a handgun shiver-and-shake area will be quite large during the first sessions of aiming practice. However, and this is the important factor in accepting the concept of aiming in the shiver-and-shake area, **shots fired with the sights correctly aligned and with proper trigger-finger motion will strike within the shiver-and-shake area.** It is as simple as that.

Accept the movement of the gun at arm's length when sighting and aiming, use extreme care in lining up the sights with each other, holding them in alignment, and concentrating on an unhurried trigger-finger pressure, and the point of impact will always be where the gun is aimed—not **away** from where it was aimed at the moment of firing.

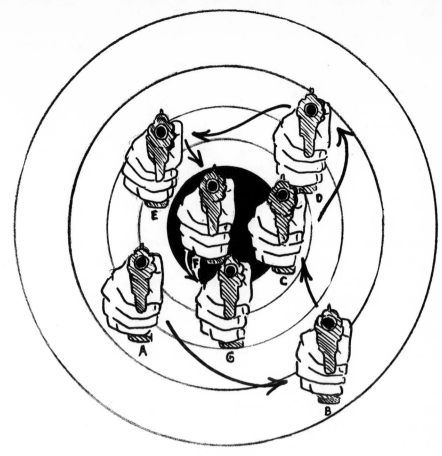

Area Aiming

No one can hold a handgun absolutely steady on an aiming **point.**
Novice shooters will swing and sway in an area approximating a
to g on target. With practice, this area can be reduced; the gun will
still swing and sway, but within an area represented by C, F, and G,
a smaller area centered on the target.

Failure to accept normal gun movement in hand-
gunnery probably resulted from the work of nonshooting
artists in illustrating older gun books, military publications,
and the charts put out by various gun companies on sighting
and aiming. The artists depicted the "ideal" when they illustrated a set of sights sitting smack under a bull's-eye
without motion of any kind. Most shooters mistakenly assumed the illustrated sight picture was attainable. Actually,
to shoot a "possible" score of 100 on a bull's-eye target only
requires the shooter to hold his aligned sights within a 3- to
5-inch circle (depending on the target), and even this apogee

of perfection does not require the motionless sight picture used in some books and charts.

The beginning shooter cannot hold in a small area because he is not as yet accustomed to the weight of the gun at the end of his arm. With normal practice, most shooters will find that their area of aiming becomes less the more they practice, until they stabilize in an area about equal to the 9-ring. It should be remembered, though, as the aiming area diminishes with increasing practice, scores will go up. A shooter whose aiming area may equal the entire diameter of the 6-ring (almost out to the edges of the target) will have a score, at the least, above 60 for ten shots; an aiming area equal to the 8-ring means a score of 80 or higher; and one equal to the diameter of the bull's-eye means all tens or a "possible"—the top score. Practice will permit many shooters to hold within a 3- or 5-inch circle. I have been area aiming for years, and at several periods during these years the development of muscular structure and nerve control enabled me to shoot "possibles."

This diminishing aiming area can be speeded up through exercises. Muscular development means the weapon can be held out at arm's length without any feeling of tension or tiredness. Since the "away" theory proves shots cannot be "horsed" into the center of a target with any regularity, then the way to reduce the normal shiver-and-shake area is through planned exercise.

Muscle Building

In handgun shooting it is not really a case of developing muscles, but a matter of training the muscles to accommodate an unusual load at the end of the arm. However, extensive physical conditioning of the muscles that control the hand and support the arm is absolutely necessary for all students of shooting. I have just recently finished a two-semester experiment in teaching shooting to five members of Sacramento State College's football team—young men in top physical condition. Their shiver-and-shake area during the first range practice sessions was identical with that of some of our regular students, but this area rapidly diminished as the muscular control of these youngsters was achieved with only a few exercises and brief range firing.

Exercises with a weight at the end of the arm will help to lessen the area in which movement occurs during the aiming-and-firing cycle. An electric iron is readily available in every home and is a fine weight for such practice. An electric drill can be utilized, and some of them even have "pistol" grips. A milk bottle filled with water can be grasped by its neck, or a specially weighted wristlet can be purchased from sporting goods stores. Do not hang any heavy object

Training wristlet. A leather and vinyl wristlet filled with lead shot to develop steadiness in musculature of arms and shoulders can be made at home or purchased at sporting goods stores. Average weight for beginners is 1½ to 2 pounds.

upon the handgun when aiming as its swing only increases the normal movement of the gun—and this is rather discouraging.

The pistol or revolver itself can be utilized for this muscle-conditioning exercise merely by holding it out for extensive periods. The advantage of holding out the handgun itself is that the sights can be lined up with some object (in a safe direction) and the gun held roughly horizontal. The

Coach Lee Kibbe demonstrating the use of the new area-aiming target. A black square instead of the regulation bull's-eye is provided for aiming. Such demonstrations, and actual practice shooting on this target, prove to student shooters the importance of the two handgun sights as primary reference points in aiming. (The ear "muffs" are for noise protection, and the training wristlet to develop the muscular structure holding the gun in aiming position.)

heavier weight of the iron, drill, and like objects will be worth the additional effort, because the pistol or revolver itself is just not heavy enough for this exercise. The wristlet mentioned above meets the problem halfway, adding a stabilized weight to the arm while it is holding the handgun. It is also possible to make a wristlet of this type at home. Only a little sewing is required, and it can be filled with bird shot or buckshot to provide the necessary weight.

When a handgun is handled for practice without firing live ammunition, it is known as "dry shooting." Dry shooting is an integral part of the learning-to-shoot process. Right now, exercise could begin with sighting and aiming practice alone—without trigger pressure snapping. Just hold the handgun at arm's length with the correct grip and sight alignment, and aim at some area. This could be a framed picture on the wall, the upper door hinge, or like target—just keep the area large at this stage. Concentration should be on sight alignment (intrasight relationship). When the hand and arm shake a great deal from tiredness, the shooter should bring back the handgun to the Raise Pistol position and rest a moment, then repeat until really tired.

At this point, put away the handgun and pick up the weight you have selected. Grasp it firmly with a grip as close to your shooting grip as possible. Extend it out at arm's length. Sight along its top and try to hold it within your target aiming area, or at least up to it. Return to Raise Pistol position when tired, and repeat—and repeat and repeat. (Rest sessions can be tied in with exercising the hand with a small ball or grip exerciser.)

These exercise sessions can also be tied in with correct breath adjustment. Your objective is to hold the small amount of breath necessary for the aiming-and-firing cycle without tension of any kind. Hold your breath when exercising and dry shooting. Remember, this must be done on the range without conscious thinking. Tie your breathing in with the extension of the arm into shooting position.

Nerve Control and Framing a Shot

Worry ruins good shooting. Believe it or not, it is worrying about firing a poor score that leads to framing a
shot. Put it another way, it is the desire to fire a top score,
quite normally, that leads to the attempt to be too precise in
looking for a sight picture (suitable for framing) that leads to
poor scores. Most psychologists will refuse to differentiate
between worrying about a poor score and desiring to shoot
a high one. There is a tie-in—you feel good when you shoot
well and bad when you shoot low scores. Authorities do
agree, however, that the fear of status loss from shooting
poorly will probably be a stronger stimulus than the desire
to excel.

Nerve control, for effective shooting, consists of a
continuous mental feedback of the creed of area aiming. It
is almost a talking-to-yourself as the gun is aimed and fired:
"Don't try to frame the shot, let it swing; just keep up that
gradual trigger pressure, watch the sights; don't try to make
it go off, let it swing, watch the sights; and keep up the
trigger-finger motion."

Nerve control is mental conditioning against doing
an act that will ruin a good score. Remember, the fear of
shooting a poor score—or the motivation to shoot better—is
always present. It never leaves the mind of a shooter on the
range or in the field. Therefore, the corrective action that safe-
guards a shooter from falling into the bad habit of framing
must be thought about as each and every shot is aimed—
otherwise the shooter gets a slight, sneaky idea he is better
than the rest of us and can make the gun go off exactly
when it is hanging on an aiming point.

Effective nerve control is achieved when the shooter
can **wait** without worry for the shot to be fired, to increase
trigger pressure steadily and hold his aligned sights in the
aiming area while he **waits** for the gun to fire. He knows he

has achieved this nerve control when there is no suspicion of hurrying the shot and no awareness the gun is **about** to fire.

The "Hold" in Area Aiming

The hold in area aiming is the area of your normal shivering-and-shaking. It is neither a "six o'clock" nor a "center" hold—that is, a point at the bottom of the bull's-eye (six o'clock) or a point in its center.

    Once the shooting arm is extended and the sights are lined up with each other, the gun and arm both settle down

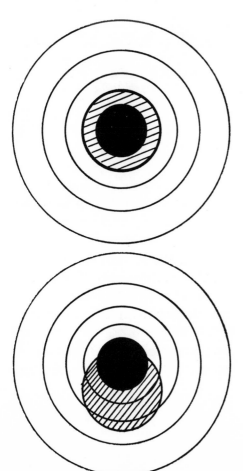

The "Hold" in Area Aiming. Top: The aiming area for guns sighted in for center "holding." **Bottom:** The aiming area for shooters who sight their guns in for a six-o'clock "hold." The area may be increased or decreased by the "holding" ability of individual shooters, but its rough center is related to sight adjustment: Shots fired when the aimed sights are swinging in the center of a shooter's aiming area should hit in the center of the bull's-eye.

into a tight movement. This is the aiming area of your hold.
A good hold is **anywhere** in this area. There cannot be any
attempt to fire shots only when the gun swings in the center
of this area, or the shooter regresses to precision-point aiming.

Most handguns can be sighted in to shoot in any
area desired. Normal factory procedure is to sight a handgun
in to shoot at the bottom of the bull's-eye, in the six o'clock
area. If you have a gun with fixed sights, your hold is within
an area whose center is the bottom of the bull's-eye. But a
good hold would be above this center (in the black of the
bull's-eye), below it, and to either side—and just how far
"out" depends on the developed ability of the shooter to hold
within a tight aiming area. If the sights can be moved, a good
adjustment for area aiming is the center hold, in which the
center of the bull's-eye is the **rough center** of the aiming area.
Many shooters prefer white space in which to aim when
shooting on paper targets and adjust their sights so the **rough
center** of their aiming area is well below the bull's-eye area
on the target.

Calling Shots

The concept of never firing a careless shot must be learned
early, when slow fire is attempted for the first time. Care
in shooting is learned from "calling the shot." To call a
shot is to note mentally just where the sights happened to be
on the target at the moment the weapon fired. Shots are
naturally expected to hit the target where aimed, and something is wrong when there is any deviation from the "call":
the expected point of impact.

The purpose of this system of locating shots on a
target is to alert the shooter when his bullets are striking

away from where he believed they were aimed at the moment the handgun fired, the spot on target of the last visual image before the shock of recoil disturbed the position of the gun.

For the purpose of calling shots, the target is divided into pie-shaped segments in accordance with the positions of the hours on a clock face. The top segment in the center is known as twelve o'clock, the bottom as six o'clock, and the mid-positions at either side as three and nine o'clock. Finer distinctions can be made by the position of the intervening hours. The second coordinate to position the point of impact of a bullet upon a target in calling shots is the distance away from the center. This can be achieved by using standard measurements, or the scoring rings of the target itself can be utilized. A hit at three o'clock can either be "2 inches" out, or "an 8 at three o'clock."

To call a shot, the shooter notes to himself immediately after firing a shot—or tells his shooting partner or coach: "A 7 at four o'clock." "Probably a 10 or a 9, just out, at six o'clock." A small replica of a target can be marked with points of impact and the target checked after firing five or ten shots. Scoping—the use of a spotting scope after each shot is fired—simplifies this procedure. The bullet holes are readily visible, and the shooter need not make any written record. This is also true of big-bore handguns as the size of the bullet hole is usually visible without a scope at short handgun ranges.

In any event, if the bullet does strike where you thought it was aimed at the moment of discharge—or within 2 or 3 inches of expectations—forget it and go on to the next shot, attempting to repeat the procedure that made the called shot strike right where you called it. On the other hand, if it did not strike in its expected location, an analysis must be made of the causes of failure. First, mentally check out your last intrasight relationship. Was the front sight squarely in the middle of the rear sight? What was your last visual impression of the lines of white? Of the relationship between the tops of the two sights? If your considered review is "good," then the fault must rest with trigger-finger motion: poor, stinking, jerky, aware-of-when-the-gun-was-about-to-fire trigger-finger pressure!

There can be no other explanation. Not if the shooter had been careful: sights held in good alignment with each other; a constant grip and tension-free position maintained. The only reasonable conclusion justified is that a sudden pressure on the trigger and possibly flinching, or both, moved the gun **away** from where it had been aimed.

This is the alert—this is the reason for calling the shot, to determine when the shot does not hit where expected. It may indicate carelessness in position or grip, sighting, or aiming, but it is usually a warning to correct faulty trigger pressure, and inherent in this warning is an implication of the need for area aiming. This is the concept that helps shooters avoid the mistake of making the gun go off by teaching an aiming process within their muscular and nerve control capability.

5

THE I-FACTORS IN
TRIGGER-FINGER MOTION

Imperceptibility
Increasing Trigger Pressure
Pacing Trigger-Finger Motion
Freezing on the Trigger
Straight-to-the-Rear Trigger Pressure
Apparent Trigger Motion

THE I-FACTORS OF EFFECTIVE TRIGGER FINGER MOTION ARE IMPERCEPTIBIL-ity, an increasing trigger pressure, and an independent grip pressure.

Imperceptibility—not knowing the handgun is about to go off—is an absolute necessity to pistol-shooting skill. An **increasing trigger pressure** will achieve this lack of awareness as to just when a handgun is about to fire. Lastly, an **independent grip pressure** guards against freezing on the grip and being unable to exert any meaningful pressure on the trigger. Area aiming is a concept that will assist a shooter in achieving the I-factors in trigger-finger motion, but the correct I-factors cannot be gained if area aiming is ignored and the pistol or revolver precision-point-aimed and the trigger "jerked" with a sudden motion.

Imperceptibility

Imperceptibility in trigger-finger motion does not come about by chance; it is the result of both determination and concentration. First, the shooter must be determined that he will not make the gun go off, that he will not let himself be "baited" by the lure of the bull's-eye and the apparently possible chance to precision-point aim. Secondly, his mental concentration should be upon sight alignment and area aiming to the **seeming** exclusion of everything else, but actually to subliminate the desire or wish to fire the shot when it is hanging on a "point" on the target (framing it). Subliminally—just under the conscious level—every effort is being made by the shooter to achieve a steadily increasing trigger pressure that will release the hammer without the

63

shooter becoming aware of the fact that it is about to be released and will fire the shot. "Surprise" when the shot goes off is the key idea. Many expert handgunners say imperceptibility results from "wishing" a shot off.

It is imperceptibility in trigger pressure that makes it possible for a shooter to hold the sights of a handgun in alignment with each other without flinching or otherwise moving the gun at the vital moment when the gun is fired and the bullet leaves the barrel.

Increasing Trigger Pressure

An increasing pressure upon the trigger means a trigger-finger motion that starts and **keeps going** until the shot is fired, without any pause or hesitancy of any kind.

Years ago, the old stop-and-go trigger pressure actually built up a marked tendency to jerk the trigger—and, of course, to flinch. The old idea of trigger motion was to **stop** the trigger pressure when your handgun moved away from your aiming point—to hold the pressure at the existing level—and then to "go" with a little more pressure when the gun moved back on its aiming point. Sounds good, and it can be accomplished most of the time, but not all of the time. Stop-and-go trigger motion results in a tight group plus several flyers: several shots low and left on the target (out of the 7-ring) from jerking or flinching, or high up and to the right in the 6- and 5-ring due to lunging forward in a "heeling" motion to meet the expected recoil.

Stop-and-go trigger-finger motion could be made to pay off in good scores on the paper target range, but it would be worse than useless in combat or hunting, when speed is required in firing the shot and **every** shot must be equally accurate. A stop-and-go trigger pressure takes time, and in

combat or in hunting, time is something precious. An attack-
ing criminal or a charging animal would upset any wait-
'em-out sequence of stop-and-go trigger-finger motion. Also,
the lack of shot-after-shot accuracy may mean death. The
one or two flyers common with this trigger pressure may be
the misses that mean disaster!

A **steadily increasing** trigger motion results in top accuracy on the pistol and revolver range for **every** shot fired.
Many shooters are often surprised to find out that their time-
fire and rapid-fire scores surpass their slow-fire scores. In
time and rapid fire a shooter fires five shots within a stated
time limit: usually 20 seconds for time fire and 10 seconds
for rapid fire. Shooter after shooter has been amazed at
the tightness of a group of ten shots fired when there was
just no time for stop-and-go trigger-finger motion, and when
the rapidity of fire demanded a steadily increasing trigger-
finger motion. It is in this characteristic of time and rapid-fire
shooting that the effectiveness of the theory of a steadily
increasing trigger motion was born—and proved.

Pacing Trigger-Finger Motion

A long time span in applying trigger-finger motion enhances
the possibility of a shooter becoming impatient and back-
sliding into making the gun go off with a sudden trigger-
finger pressure.

Once the ability to fire one shot in slow fire has been
achieved, the gun should be held out at arm's length for a
second shot. The first effort after recovering from the recoil
of the preceding shot is to fight to bring the gun back down
on the target. If a revolver is being fired single action, this
is when the hammer is cocked. As the gun settles down on
the line of sight, the shooter draws the front sight into align-

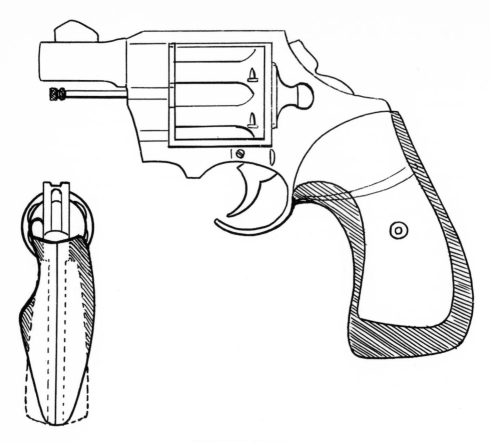

CUSTOM GRIPS

The hand-filling characteristics of made-to-measure grips to fit the hands
of individual shooters aid in developing a rapid cadence in shooting
heavy-caliber handguns by preventing the "climb" or "creep" of the gun
in the shooter's hand from shot to shot. Shaded areas indicate the new
dimensions of custom grips beyond the normal measurements of factory
stocks, and dotted lines indicate areas in which the dimensions have been
reduced. Stocks illustrated were designed by Chic Gaylord of New York
City for combat shooting.

Below: Two custom grips by Steve Herrett of Twin Falls, Idaho. The
uncheckered model on the K-series Smith and Wesson .38 revolver is a
set of Presentation stocks; the checkered grips on the Ruger .357 Magnum
Blackhawk are Herrett's Shooting Star model, a popular design with
shooters in America.

ment with the rear sight **anywhere on the target,** and **at the same time** moves the entire gun and hastily aligned sights over and into the aiming area. At this moment, the initial pressure is placed upon the trigger, as the sights fall into proper alignment with each other. Trigger pressure is **steadily** increased as the sights are more carefully aligned and held in alignment—until the weapon fires without any perception on the part of the shooter except an attention to the sights and to a continuing of the trigger pressure.

Learning how to recover the aiming picture promptly and using it to pace the time of trigger-finger motion are important for all shooting, even slow fire. This is based upon the idea that a concentration upon one task will lead to a conditioning to perform a necessary accompanying and related task.

Actually it is these "second" shots during initial practice sessions that lead to proper timing for the first shot, or any slow-fire shot. Aiming may be slightly slower on the first shot because the gun must be extended up and into the line of sight, rather than just bounced back after recoil at arm's length. However, the time span in the trigger-finger motion of second shots is soon carried over into pacing trigger motion for the first shot.

Each shot is called and neither shot is fired carelessly, but once the first shot is fired (and called), the shooter must forget it and concentrate on the second shot. Then, after both shots have been fired, the calls for each shot can be checked with actual points of impact.

A fast-paced trigger pressure is invaluable when shooting against the time limits of rapid and time fire, in attempting to knock down an animal in the hunting field, or against the time limit inherent in an armed opponent firing a rapid return fire. This learning to time trigger-finger motion with the recovery of the aiming picture will also be invaluable in achieving a **cadence** of equal time between shots and an ability to achieve the same discrimination in sighting and aiming from shot to shot—almost a guarantee of shot-to-shot accuracy.

Freezing on the Trigger

Freezing on a trigger describes the plight of a marksman who cannot seem to exert sufficient pressure upon the trigger of a handgun to fire the shot because of misdirecting pressure to the grip. This unfortunate shooter fights against an apparently heavy and abnormal trigger pressure: The trigger seems to require apparent pressures of 20 to 100 pounds. The shooter squeezes the grip with pounds and pounds of pressure, but the trigger finger is immobile. That is, it is motionless until the shooter becomes desperate at the great weight of the trigger and his inability to fire the gun, and exerts a sudden and convulsive trigger motion to fire the gun.

    The shooter's index finger on the trigger cannot respond when the major muscles of his hand are in conflict. There is no trigger-finger movement, but it **seems** that pounds and pounds of pressure are being put on the trigger when in fact the pressure is being exerted upon the grip.

    Learn what to expect of your trigger motion. Learn its normal weight by snapping the hammer on an empty chamber or fired cartridge case in dry firing. Look for this same weight in trigger pressure when the handgun is loaded and aimed on the range. There is no reason for one shot to have a greater trigger pressure than another, or for trigger pressure to vary when shots are fired as against trigger pressure when the handgun is empty. Testing for freezing must be constant—be alert to it whenever the trigger seems heavier than normal or a feeling of impatience is noted.

    An effective safeguard is to pace trigger-finger motion

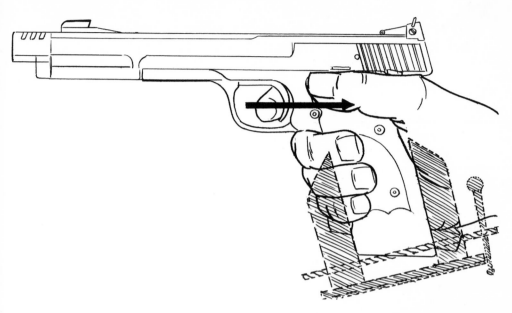

Trigger Pressure. Only the trigger finger moves; and this motion is straight to the rear. The viselike grip of the remaining fingers of the hand remains constant with no increase or decrease in grip pressure. This is a steadily increasing pressure until the weapon fires; it is not a stop-and-go pressure; and there is a need for imperceptibility: the firing of the gun must surprise the shooter. Any awareness that a handgun is **about to fire** causes movement at the vital moment of firing and destroys accuracy.

carefully and to be alerted to this freezing potential when the time span of trigger motion appears to lengthen. Positive thinking is to concentrate on building up trigger pressure steadily while grip pressure is held to an unchanging constancy.

Straight-to-the-Rear Trigger Pressure

Trigger-finger pressure to one side often develops and can add pounds to a trigger pull and result in a "freezing" similar to squeezing on the grip instead of putting pressure on the trigger. This may be detracted by a "creep" or unevenness in the trigger motion that results from the trigger being pressed sideways against the uneven surfaces of its housing within the frame of the pistol or revolver. This is readily differentiated from a mechanical defect as it occurs only now and then—when side pressure is exerted on the trigger.

The best method of controlling any tendency to putting side pressure on the trigger is to concentrate on straight-to-the-rear trigger pressure. Think of a spot on the palm of your shooting hand, just to the rear of the index finger's contact point on the trigger and try to "touch" this spot as you press the trigger. This helps to direct trigger movement toward a point straight to the rear of the initial trigger movement.

Apparent Trigger Motion

Three common forms of apparent trigger motion exist, and they are all detrimental to achieving effective I-factors in pistol and revolver shooting.

These mechanical defects which will roadblock attempts of a shooter to develop an imperceptible, increasing, and independent trigger motion are termed: (1) slack, (2) creep, and (3) backslap.

Trigger Slack—This is the initial movement of the trigger before pressure is exerted upon the firing mechanism —the "free" movement of the trigger before it actually starts to function. Slack is not usually encountered when shooting a revolver, but it may be found on military-type handguns, such as the Colt .45 automatic pistol. Coaches in pistol marksmanship, many years ago, taught trigger-finger motion by instructing shooters: "Take up the slack right away, **now** the trigger pressure." Many new shooters, however, acquire a handgun with this trigger slack. Knowing little about the need to take it up promptly and forget it, they "squeeze" this slack and never learn effective trigger pressure. If any handgun has this free movement in its trigger motion at the beginning of the trigger pull, the slack must be taken up promptly and firmly before the actual trigger pressure. If it is a slack that does not have an easily detected range, the gun should be taken to a skilled gunsmith for corrective action.

Trigger Creep—Any easily perceived trigger movement is usually termed a creep in the trigger. It may be a slight unevenness in the trigger movement due to roughness of the moving parts of the gun activating the firing mechanism; a definite grinding motion that occurs when minute pieces of grit find their way between these moving metal surfaces; or it may be a skipping motion that occurs when the surfaces of these gun parts become rounded or grooved. Any kind of creep makes it almost impossible to achieve the necessary **imperceptibility** of the trigger-finger motion.

A trigger creep makes it difficult to hold the sights in alignment, destroys a shooter's ability to concentrate on sight alignment and trigger motion, and leads to a habit of sudden trigger pressures by the unevenness of its motion.

Trigger Backslap—Gunsmiths can also correct backslap: excessive trigger movement after the hammer or firing pin is released. Test for backslap by holding the empty gun at "Raise Pistol" position with the thumb of the nonshooting hand holding some pressure on the hammer spur. This pressure is just enough to let the hammer move forward when the trigger releases it, but firm enough to hold it in the just-released position. When the hammer is released, hold it **at that point** with thumb pressure, and swing back on the trigger. Carefully observe if there is any motion to the trigger **after** it has released the hammer. If more motion than is necessary to release the firing mechanism is detected, the gun has backslap. Excessive movement of the trigger in backslap has a tendency to speed up trigger-finger motion so that a slap occurs when the trigger stops its motion. The longer the trigger movement in this backslap, the greater the slapping motion against the gun—and the greater the possibility of disturbing the sight alignment and aiming of the gun at the really vital moment—when the bullet is about to leave the barrel.

6

DOUBLE-ACTION SHOOTING

Two-Stage Double Action
Straight-Through Trigger Pressure
The Grip in Double-Action Shooting
"Milking" the Trigger

MODERN REVOLVERS CAN BE FIRED EITHER SINGLE OR DOUBLE ACTION. In single-action firing the shooter cocks the hammer with his thumb; in double-action shooting the hammer is cocked and the cylinder turned—and the gun fired—solely by trigger-finger pressure. In utilizing the trigger to wheel back the hammer into a ready-to-fire position, and to turn the cylinder to place a live cartridge in front of the firing pin, the shooter must press the trigger through about a half inch of motion and an apparent 10 to 15 pounds of pressure. In comparison, the single-action trigger pull has no apparent motion, and pressure of 2½ to 4½ pounds on the trigger will fire most revolvers. It is little wonder the beginning shooter favors single-action shooting.

Double-Action Shooting Is Speed Shooting. This .38 Colt Cobra has the front of its trigger guard cut away and the hammer despurred for top speed.

Many years ago, double-action shooting was considered a waste of ammunition. The aftereffect of placing about 15 pounds of trigger pressure moved the aimed handgun away from its aiming area at the moment of firing, and most shooters could not hit the target. Those were the days of the creed of "Better one aimed shot than several misses." A few expert shooters, however, firmly believed that the speed of double-action shooting made its use mandatory in combat shooting and worked hard at its development.

Ed McGivern's fine landmark research in this field of marksmanship demonstrated that "fast and fancy" revolver shooting could be achieved only by shooting double-action. Ed, who fired six shots from a .38 revolver into a playing card at 18 feet within **nine-tenths of a second,** shooting double-action, wrote in his fine book, **Fast and Fancy Revolver Shooting:** "The reason for firing revolvers by the double-action method is based entirely on the urge and the need for speed. Persistent practice and prolonged tests have shown conclusively that greater accuracy can be combined with speed by this method than by any other method by which revolvers have ever been operated." However, it was not until the Federal Bureau of Investigation initiated its Practical Pistol Course that double-action shooting became popular. Up until that time, a premium had been placed upon slow-fire accuracy with a bull's-eye target, and it was not until this leading law enforcement agency pioneered in using silhouette (man-shaped) targets under combat conditions that double action came to the attention of serious shooters. It was, as McGivern had said, a "need for speed."

Double-action shooting is popular among police officers shooting combat courses of fire and among civilian shooters who utilize it for target shooting. Most double-action men have learned a two-stage trigger pull, but many of them shoot with the straight-through trigger motion. In either case, the modern double-action shooters have learned to control the long and heavy trigger motion necessary to the mechanics of cocking the hammer and turning the cylinder with trigger pressure, and today they even threaten the supremacy of single-action shooters on the target range.

Double-action shooting can be learned, and it offers accuracy equal to the best of single-action shooting, and the ability to shoot rapid fire **fast.**

Two-Stage Double Action

The two-stage trigger motion in double-action revolver shooting involves a sweeping movement of the trigger finger to the rear for about two-thirds of the full trigger movement, and a squeezing or easing of pressure for the remaining third. In effect, most of the apparent motion and weight of the trigger is taken up in the first motion of the two-stage trigger pull, and the second stage of this trigger pressure is very similar to any single-action trigger motion.

Most shooters utilize a "pressure point" to locate the end point of the first stage of this type of trigger pressure. This is the point the tip of the trigger finger touches when it is about two-thirds of the way through its trigger motion in double-action shooting. It may be the rear edge of the trigger guard, the frame of the gun just above the rear of trigger guard, the edge of a built-up grip, or even the tip of the shooter's thumb as it grips the gun. The contact of trigger fingertip with the pressure point serves to warn the shooter to hold his sweeping-back motion, and to start a trigger pressure that will ease into a smooth let-off with the same imperceptibility as in single-action and autopistol shooting.

However, many double-action shooters also utilize the pressure point to cushion trigger-finger pressure at the time the hammer is released, starts to fall, and fires the cartridge. In action, the shooter continues his trigger pressure when the tip of his index finger touches the pressure point, allowing the tip of his finger to slide along the pressure point as final pressure is placed upon the trigger. This cushioning of trigger-finger pressure in the second stage of two-stage double-action revolver shooting aids the mechanical trigger stop in preventing trigger backslap from destroying the aim of the weapon at the vital moment just before the bullet leaves the barrel.

Practice can develop a truly amazing ability in the trigger finger of any shooter, and this is in both the strength to apply a heavy trigger pull and the discrimination as to when to ease off into a steadily increasing trigger pressure. Actually, the entire double-action trigger motion is a steadily increasing pressure. The first stage is mechanical and always the same: a fast, sweeping motion to the rear until the tip of the trigger finger touches its pressure point; while the second stage is devoted to a steady increase in existing trigger pressure **and a waiting for the gun to fire**—just as in single-action or autopistol shooting.

Straight-Through Trigger Pressure

A straight-through trigger pressure in double-action revolver shooting may appear to be more difficult than two-stage trigger pressure at first, but it also can be mastered with the same tools: work and concentration. Again, it is a case of developing strength and some discrimination in the trigger finger. The apparent lack of control in the straight-through trigger pressure forces the marksman to work hard in developing a trigger-finger motion that will not move the sights out of alignment either while pressure is being exerted upon the trigger or at the vital moment of hammer release—when the bullet is about to leave the weapon.

Since straight-through pressure does not have the

"braking factor" inherent in the pressure point of two-stage trigger-finger motion, it is necessary for the shooter to learn to put the final pressure on the trigger without the "bumping" motion common to the old days of double-action shooting. The energy resulting from putting about 15 pounds of pressure on the trigger cannot be suddenly released against the frame of the gun in such a manner that the consequent "bump" moves the aimed sights just as the gun is about to be fired. Muscular control can be developed to hold back on most of this pressure as the trigger releases the hammer for its forward fall and the firing of the cartridge, and the remaining pressure can be dissipated harmlessly—**so long as the trigger pressure is straight to the rear the sights will not bob or dip at the moment of hammer release.**

Trigger control in learning to hold the sights in alignment during a straight-through double-action trigger pressure requires practice with the empty gun while dry shooting. It is a simple exercise, and nothing more than releasing the trigger finger forward with the same timing in which the trigger had been moved to the rear. It is a matter of lining up the sights, keeping them in alignment while putting on the pressure until the hammer falls, **and holding them in alignment as the trigger is released to its forward position.** Try it several times. Keep the sights in alignment throughout the entire process of putting pressure toward the rear on the trigger to fire the shot, and then releasing the trigger pressure with a forward motion of the trigger finger. This exercise develops a difficult-to-learn ability to hold the sights in alignment despite any slight bump at the moment of hammer release and cartridge ignition as the shot is fired.

The Grip in Double-Action Shooting

Most shooters, but particularly those with small hands, will find that the hand must be moved slightly to the right of the grip when shooting double action. When shooting "two-stage" double action a shooter must reach into the trigger guard with the trigger finger so that the fingertip will touch the reference point on the gun that is to be used as a pressure point. When shooting with a straight-through trigger motion in double action, a shooter will find it helpful to get a good portion of his index finger on the trigger as it is helpful in manipulating the trigger.

In either type of trigger motion it is highly desirable that the shooter reach down with his trigger finger to the lowest possible point on the revolver's trigger. Remember, the weight of a double-action trigger pull is about three times that of a single-action trigger pull, and the lower the finger on the trigger, the greater the leverage that can be exerted. In this connection, one of the strange things about double-action shooting is that a shooter must adjust his grip to a trigger-finger motion that reaches its high point of necessary pressure about two-thirds of the way through the entire trigger motion. This is unlike the "feel" of either single-action or autopistol trigger motions and does require a firm grip

The Combat Grip in Revolver Shooting. The thumb is down in a locked position as the weapon is fired double-action, and it is not necessary to cock the hammer with the thumb for each shot. Shooters with small hands may move their hand to favor one side of the grip in order to reach the trigger in its full forward position. This is an excellent grip for **pointability** and to hold a heavy-caliber handgun on target when fired rapidly.

with a constantly firm grip pressure, neither increasing nor decreasing throughout the trigger-finger motion.

The shooter's thumb usually rides low on the gun in double action. In fact, the high-riding thumb position of revolver shooters, in which the thumb is almost alongside the hammer, developed from the need to cock the hammer with the thumb for each shot when shooting single action. It saves a great deal of time to move the thumb only about a quarter of an inch, from its high position, than to move it an inch or more from the low position. In double-action firing the thumb can be locked down on the frame of the gun and **held there through a five-shot string.** It is a locked, thumbs-down grip, in which the only thing that moves is the index finger of the shooter.

It is difficult to describe the feeling of satisfaction when locking the thumb in place and not moving it between shots. There appears to be twice as much time available for recovering the aim after firing a shot. Cadence and trigger pacing—the regular spacing of shots no matter how fast a string of five or six shots are fired—is easily attained. The trigger motion seems to blend with recovering from the effect of recoil, and the pacing of the trigger motion is keyed to the recovery of the aiming picture. The sights almost fall into a hasty alignment, the gun is easily moved over into the aiming area, and the sights are readily aligned with each other more carefully while the gun is swinging in the aiming area—and while the shooter is continuing the steadily increasing trigger pressure.

"Milking" the Trigger

A convulsive tightening on the grip of the gun at the time of putting pressure on the trigger in double-action revolver shooting, often accompanied with an inexplicable "throwing down" of the gun, is generally termed "milking." Strangely, it is not unlike the movement of the hand used by dairy farmers, or the motion seen in modern milking machines in cow barns.

Milking the trigger includes all the faults of single-action revolver and autopistol shooting rolled up into one massive fault. The time of ignition of a handgun can be perceived quite readily by a shooter milking a trigger in double action, and the strange throwing-down motion is probably a combined punching forward to meet the expected recoil plus some movement from the suddenly increased grip pressure.

Shooting can be accurate in double action. It can also be much faster than single action, or even automatic pistol firing. It can be fired either with the two-stage trigger pull or with the straight-through trigger motion. However, accuracy is still dependent upon a trigger-finger motion that is independent of grip pressure, steadily increasing, imperceptible, and does not end up with a sudden aim-destroying "bump."

Any marksman can learn to shoot double action, so long as he remembers that any motion on the trigger that moves the weapon at the moment of firing can only move it **away** from where it had been aimed.

7

DIRECTED FIRE FROM THE HIP

Visual Cues
Pointing Is Aiming
The Grip and Position in Directed Fire
Rapid Trigger-Finger Motion

DIRECTED FIRE FROM THE HIP IS DOUBLE-ACTION **EMERGENCY** SHOOTING. There is no time to aim. The emergency may be a charging animal or an armed opponent. One may be closing fast, the other about to use knife, gun, or club. Police officers call this defensive shooting. It occurs when there is a fear of mortal injury, and prompt action is the only defense. It is a skill that can be learned, and it offers a great deal of personal satisfaction in the learning process.

The Triology of Hip Shooting. Looking . . . Pointing . . . Trigger Pressure. Practice develops the **pointability** factor, a response to visual cues, and a rapid-but-smooth trigger pressure will fire the gun as it is pointed at the target.

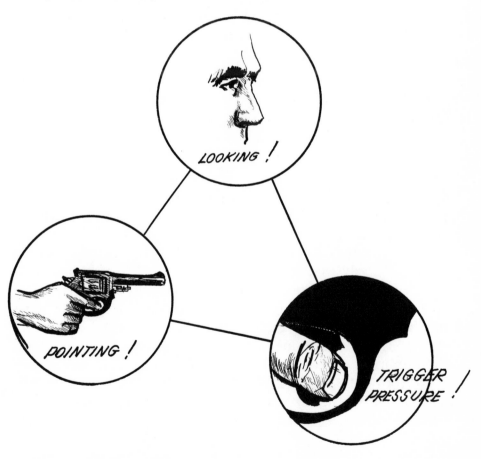

Hip shooting is confined to short distances. It is "room-sized" shooting. The Federal Bureau of Investigation's Practical Pistol Course limits shooting from the hip to seven yards. This range was determined as the result of several surveys among police units as to the distances at which gunfights actually take place. In fact, most of them are within knife-fighting range.

Shooting from the hip is instinctive shooting. It requires nothing more than training the musculature of the body and its controlling nervous system to respond to visual cues. Skilled shotgunners have used instinctive shooting for many years. They look at their flying targets, bring the gun up to where they are looking, and blast the target out of the air. Visual concentration on their flying targets directs the fire. The marksmen do not sight and aim the shotgun.

Visual Cues

The visual cues around which the necessary coordination of nerves and muscle must be developed for directing fire from the hip with accuracy almost equal to aimed fire is nothing more than the basic line of sight and great visual concentration. It can be summed up in the admonition: "Look—and look **hard!**" However, it is just a normal line of sight as taught throughout this text. It is more concentrated, and it is not permitted to waver throughout the draw-and-shoot period. It is looking at an area you want to hit **very much**—more than anything else at the moment.

This visual concentration makes it possible to point the gun instinctively, so that the "point of aim" coincides on the target with the line of sight. The weapon is not within the shooter's primary vision—that is reserved for the target —but it can be seen just at the edge of the field of secondary vision. The shooter does not look down to see where the handgun is pointing. To do so would ruin visual concentration. It is this looking **hard** at the target that makes it possible to point, punch, or throw the muzzle of the gun toward the target so that the bullets strike in the area of visual concentration.

Pointing Is Aiming

A mirror and a tennis ball are devices by which any student-shooter can develop the ability to point where he is looking. Sounds odd. They are effective teaching aids, however.

A mirror reflects the actions of the shooter. Stand in front of one. Pick out an aiming area on the mirror—on your reflected image—and look at it—**hard!** Now swing your

MIRROR TRAINING

A mirror practice target develops **pointing** ability in hip shooting. A 12-inch mirror can be fastened over a man-sized silhouette target, and the shooter can observe just where his handgun is pointing as he drops into the crouch position for hip shooting.

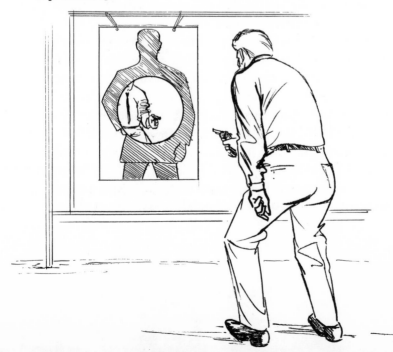

shooting hand up and forward to point at your aiming area.
Hold it! Check in the mirror and make minor adjustments.
Try it again—and again. Now, pick up your handgun. Check
it to make certain it is empty (there are rumors of seven-
years of bad luck for breaking mirrors). Repeat the pointing,
and the corrections. Try to improve each time the gun is
swept up in the pointing motion by making certain the
muzzle is pointed where you are looking.

Some shooter-students find it advantageous to think
of this pointing motion as a "throwing" or "punching"
motion, similar to throwing a ball or a punch at an object.
Ideally, if the target was in reach of the outstretched hand,
the gun's muzzle would punch a hole in the target in the
center of the selected aiming area—the area of visual concentration.

Later, this practice can be made more realistic
through the use of wax bullets, available in any sporting
goods store. Avoid plastic bullets; there is a little too much
bounce in their rebound for this type of short-range defensive shooting. Also available, along with the wax bullets,
is a simple and inexpensive tool for knocking out the old
primer (the ignition device in the cartridge base) and insert-
ing a new one. Wax bullets need no powder for this practice because the energy in the blast-off of the primer is
sufficent to send the wax projectile on an accurate though
short flight to its mirror target.

In shooting wax bullets at a mirrored reflection, the
results are scored by looking for the visual impact and wax
smudge. If the impact was close to where the shooter had
been looking and striving to hit, then it would be scored as
a hit. Wax-bullet shooting offers a real opportunity to learn
how to direct fire from the hip with accuracy. Work hard at
achieving perfection. Watch the point of impact of each shot,
then make the necessary corrections from shot to shot, from
gun load to gun load. From time to time, change the aiming
area to another portion of your reflected image. Fire several

rounds at this new aiming area. Rest. Clean off the wax smudges on the mirror with solvent and a rag. Shoot again —and again.

The tennis ball is unusual and you may wish to skip it. I chanced on it back in 1958 when doing research for my book, **Combat Shooting for Police.** One of the police officers in Hollywood, Florida, did remarkable well on "first shot" practice in combat gunnery sessions. A brief interrogation as to this officer's uncanny pointing skill met with evasive answers. Finally, he admitted that throwing a tennis ball at a mark on his garage door "grooved" an underhand swing for the draw-and-shoot practice.

Drawing a pistol from a hip holster and pointing it accurately can be reduced to a smooth underhand motion, and the same motion can be stylized through the use of a ball with a mark on any wall to delineate an aiming area. If the ball strikes high—or low—the shot fired from a similar swing up-and-forward when hip shooting with a handgun would also have been high—or low.

Pointing is aiming, and akin to throwing and punching. The mirror is an effective teaching device as it reflects a man-shaped image of the shooter—a perfect target for combat gunnery. Wax bullets are the newest teaching aid for hip shooting. And sneak in a little ball-throwing practice just to test swinging ability.

The Grip and Position in Directed Fire

The grip in directed fire from the hip is the same as in double-action shooting, except that the initial grasping of the gun is done in the holster, before the handgun is drawn. Any juggling of the gun to change the grip as the weapon moves up and out of the holster and forward in its pointing motion really ruins nerve and muscular response to visual cues.

The handgun is gripped firmly **in the holster** for hip shooting. This initial graspng is accomplished with the three lower fingers of the hand. As the handgun is drawn upward, the thumb is brought to a firm resting place on the side of the gun. And as the weapon sweeps forward (clear of the buttock, thigh, knee, and the feet of the shooter), the index finger is inserted in the trigger guard and the trigger-finger motion started to the rear.

The grip in hip shooting should be a very firm grip, or at least sufficiently firm to tighten without tension the muscles in the wrist and arm of the shooter. It is this increased firmness of the grip that holds the handgun on target from shot to shot. Of course, the shooter strives to bring the gun back to its original pointing position in recovering from the recoil of the preceding shot, and also works hard to hold it there—motionless—during the time of trigger motion, but it is the firm grip that really bounces the gun back after each shot.

The hip-shooting position is assumed by taking a short step to the left, spreading the feet for balance; dropping the buttocks down as the knees are flexed and the body bent **slightly** forward, and distributing the body's weight evenly on both feet.

This crouch position achieves target reduction (over 30 percent), but its primary purpose is to compress the body structure and make a shooter much more responsive to visual cues than he would be in a normal standing position. This position permits a shooter to fire from the hip with a "locked unit" from the muzzle of his gun to his shoulder. The barrel of the handgun and the forearm of the shooter will be in a horizontal plane, roughly parallel to the ground. This is not a sought-after position, but a natural result of the pointing, throwing, or punching motion of the gun toward the target.

The Crouch Position for Hip Shooting. In hip shooting top accuracy is achieved by responding to visual cues. The shooter **looks** at his target and **points** his handgun. Dropping into a crouch position relaxes the muscular structure of the body and allows immediate response to the visual cue of looking at the target. It is a position of controlled relaxation in which the buttocks are dropped downward, the knees flexed, and the upper body inclined forward slightly in order to place the center of gravity of the entire body just over the feet.

Developing a Stable Position for Hip Shooting. Shooting a handgun "where you are looking" shot after shot demands a stable position; not only is there a need for **pointability** in getting off the first shot, but there is also a need for holding the gun on target for the next shot. A three-point procedure for developing a stable position is: (1) buttocks dropped down; (2) forearm and gun barrel parallel to the ground, and forearm and hand locked into one **pointing** unit by a firm grip which tightens up the wrist muscles; and (3) elbow tucked into body to bring the gun directly under the line of sight.

Below right: Curtis W. Fuller, Technical Assistant, Sacramento State College, demonstrates a stable hip-shooting position. Note position of gun directly under the line of sight.

2. — FOREARM AND GUN BARREL PARALLEL TO GROUND —

3. — ELBOW IN TOWARD CENTER —

1. BUTTOCKS DROPPED DOWN —

The compressed body structure is utilized as a bipod. Changes in elevation are made by moving up or down in the crouch (at the knees), and horizontal corrections are made by swinging the entire body to one side or the other. This bipod procedure avoids the old fault of overcorrection, which was quite common when pointing faults were corrected by flexion at the wrist or elbow.

When the visual concentration exists at the necessary level of intensity, there is no head movement of any kind. The shooter is alerted to a hazard in real life. He looks at it, recognizes the danger and his need to respond, and brings his gun up to point where he has been looking. Despite body movements in crouching, or correcting from shot to shot, the head is not bent downward or sideways. The eyes of the shooter are glued to the area in which he intends to place the shots, and once in the bipod shooting position, the only moving portion of the body is the trigger finger.

Rapid Trigger-Finger Motion

In hip shooting with a handgun, the trigger must be pressed rapidly in double action to secure the necessary lifesaving speed of fire. It is a straight-through double-action trigger pressure, and there is no time for any two-stage trigger pull. However, the **away** theory still functions in hip shooting. The trigger must be pressed in such a fashion that the gun is not moved **away** from where it had been pointed. This is the most common fault in hip shooting.

Milking the trigger is the easiest trigger fault to detect, the convulsive tightening on the grip as the trigger is pressed and the throwing-down motion of the gun can be observed by any shooter. Self-analysis starts with misses on the target and extends to the actual mechanics of trigger pressure.

It is a thinking-back device in which honesty is vital. Was there any feeling of movement just before the shot was fired?

Less open to detection is the habit of bumping the trigger-finger motion when the trigger releases the hammer and just before the bullet leaves the barrel. Alertness to this fault requires real concentration at the moment of hammer release—just before the shot is fired.

The mirror used for pointing practice is also an effective teaching device for trigger-finger motion in hip shooting. Draw the empty gun, swing it up and take the crouch position, fire it rapidly several times dry shooting at the mirror image. **Watch the muzzle of the gun!** If it moves in any direction during the trigger-finger motion or upon hammer release, fight to correct it. Learn to move the trigger finger through this straight-back trigger motion without milking or bumping.

Seek cadence in trigger motion in hip shooting, try for an even pacing of the trigger pressure by aligning it with recovery from recoil. Rap off the shots in a measured tempo. Remember, terrific handgun accuracy from the hip position can be gained without sighting and aiming; merely by looking, pointing, and shooting. The shooter's body can be trained to respond to visual cues, but this response is meaningless unless the correct trigger pressure is applied at the moment of firing.

8

READING THE TARGET

ANY HANDGUN SHOOTING FAULT CAN BE CORRECTED. THEREFORE ANY shooter can improve his skill with the pistol or revolver. Corrective action, however, must depend upon a shooter's personal skill at the diagnosis of shooting faults. No one can correct a nebulous fault; the cause of poor shooting must be discovered before any attempt to correct or remove the cause is at all possible.

Diagnosis starts with the point of impact of each bullet fired. Targets can be "read." They are the communication media by which a shooter learns his faults. Each bullet hole will tell its story to the knowledgeable shooter.

Initially, the shooter must distinguish between bullets that hit where they are called and those that do not. Shots striking where they are called are an indication that a shooter has mastered the concepts of area aiming and the I-factor in correct trigger pressure and can move on to remedial action directed at reducing the size of the aiming area; but shots striking **away** from where they had been called indicates the shooter's remedial action must be directed at faults in sight alignment, aiming, or trigger pressure—or some combination of such faults.

The Called Shot

If a bullet strikes a target where it was called—where the shooter anticipated it would hit because of his last microsecond look at the sights just before the cartridge fired and the bullet started on its flight—then there is no fault to find with either sighting and aiming or trigger-finger motion.

There is fault to find with position, grip, and a muscular system not well enough developed to hold a gun out at

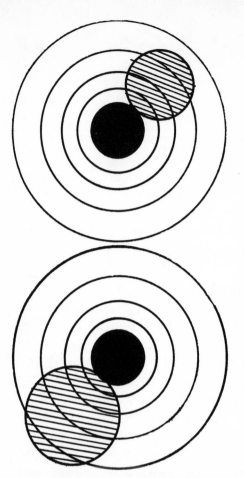

Reading the Target

Top: Shots high on the target are an indication of pushing forward to meet the recoil of the handgun. This "heeling" (trigger jerking) results from an awareness the weapon is about to fire. Right-hand shooters will heel their shots to the right as indicated by shaded area on target.

Bottom: Shots low on the target result from a punching forward to meet an expected recoil motion of the handgun. This "flinching" results from and is often joined with trigger jerking. Right-hand shooters flinch and jerk their shots into the left lower area shaded on the target.

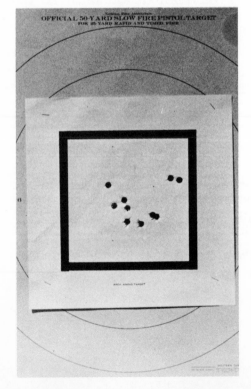

A-A Target

The author developed this "AA" target by reversing a regular bull's-eye target and pasting a square of black target pasters in its center. It was used in coaching students at Sacramento State College as an antiflinch and antijerk device. It is a 7-inch square outlined in black. The shooter concentrates on sight alignment and holds the gun within the black square on the target. Since there is no "point" of aim on this target, the shooter looks at his sights and develops correct trigger pressure, and accuracy improves. A few sessions on this target and shooters can transfer their new skills to the bull's-eye target.

arm's length. These are causative factors when a **well-aimed shot** is fired with an **excellent trigger let-off** and ends up far from the center of the target, or at least on the edges of the 7-ring.

Unnecessary tension sets up tremors in the shooter's arm that establish a shooting area much too large for accuracy, or a shooting area marked by ghostlike "nudges" somewhere in the muscular or nervous system of the shooter that make the gun dart up or down or to one side or the other in what is best described as an elliptical overlay on a normal aiming area.

When a shot is fired and called at the microsecond the sights of a handgun are on the edge of a wide aiming area, or when it seemed to dart out beyond even the normally wide aiming area, then the shooter must work to develop his ability to hold a pistol or revolver at arm's length without muscular tension. This means daily exercise with a weight, pushing it out and holding it the same way the handgun is extended and aimed. It also means almost daily dry shooting with the handgun. Both combine to cut down any shooter's wide aiming area and "darting" proclivities.

Body tensions in the basic position, or in the grip, may also be the cause of excessive movement when aiming.

Tension in any portion of the body can cause a shivering-and-shaking far beyond a normal wavering. Check the shooting position; evaluate it from the top down. Is your head erect, neck without tension? Is your elbow neither bent or locked? Is your nonshooting arm in the side pants pocket? Is the weight of your body just slightly forward, not unbalanced toward the rear? Are your feet spread a comfortable distance apart? Is there any tension in the knee area? This review must be similar to that of a pilot in checking out a list of landing procedures. Every item is to be checked out by the shooter, and a mental response made in regard to each section of the body.

A physical examination, as well as a mental check, can be made of the grip. A shooter can simulate his shooting grip at the "Raise Pistol" position and, by turning the gun over slightly, examine it closely. Again, work from top to bottom. Is the thumb placed firmly against the frame of the gun, and in the same place for each shot? Are the middle and ring fingers gripping the gun in a fore-and-aft pressure (front to rear, and with only a "holding" pressure with the fleshy base of the thumb and the palm of the hand)? Look for the signs of an incorrect digging-in pressure on the grip: the white half-moons under the tips of the fingernails. Is the little finger exerting more than its share of pressure on the grip—in comparison with the strength (firmness) of the remainder of the grip? Remember, these faults do not "throw" shots away from where they were called, but they do set up tension tremors that will increase the normal shiver-and-shake area of any shooter.

The Miscalled Shot

A miscalled shot is one that does not hit where it was called. These are the "flyers" from a tight group; these are the shots composing the "second" group **away** from the group of called shots; and these are the shots that may often make up the entire group. The miscalled shot is the inexplicable, difficult-to-understand point of impact: "How the devil did it get down there?"

Standard remedial action starts with a mental check of the sight alignment. Have you really been **watching** the sights, looking **at** them and not **through** them? Has the top of the front sight been leveled off evenly with the top of either side of the rear notch? Are the **lines of white** of the same "fatness" on either side of the front sight? Is the gun canted and are the tops of both sights not on the necessary horizontal level? If these reference points all check out satisfactorily, then the shot should have hit right where it was called—where the aligned sights appeared to be at the moment the shot was fired. The alert to faulty sight alignment is a general dispersion of shots on the target, absolutely no primary or secondary grouping, just sort of a "Swiss-cheese" target pattern.

When errors in sight alignment have been excluded as the possible cause of flyers or miscalled shots, then the trouble must be with the trigger-finger motion. A shooter can be **wrong** in three identifiable ways in connection with trigger-finger motion. Each wrong way in regard to trigger pressure puts shots in a specific place on a target: (1) Sudden pressure on the trigger (jerking) usually moves the point of impact down and to the left, about halfway out at seven o'clock; (2) Flinching (pushing forward to meet the **whoom** of the ignition of the cartridge and the kick of the recoil) moves the point of impact downward and well out; and (3) "Heeling" the gun upward and to the right by pushing forward to meet the blast and kick with the fleshy portion of the thumb and the heel of the hand flips the shots about halfway out at two o'clock.

The correction of improper trigger pressure requires a determination not to be baited into framing a shot and making the gun go off, and an equal determination to forget the bull's-eye and concentrate on letting the aligned sights swing about the aiming area while the trigger is pressed straight to the rear with a steadily increasing trigger pressure. A trigger pressure that maintains the theme of **imperceptibility**—of always being a little surprised at the exact moment of handgun ignition—must be achieved.

The Warning of the Sixth Shot

Most handgun range practice, or even "plinking," should be fired in two strings of five shots each, for a total of ten shots. The scoring rings on handgun targets have a value of 10 for the bull's-eye. Ten rounds provide a nice and neat "possible" of 100 on any pistol and revolver target. In plinking, two five-shot strings provide the shooter wishing to diagnose his own faults the traditional sixth shot of handgunners.

Experienced shooters are often quite conscious that they have fired the last shot in their handguns, and do not usually let the hammer fall on an unexpectedly empty chamber. They do sometimes, though, and the beginning shooter does it almost every gun load. When it does happen, it is an excellent opportunity to ascertain how the trigger pressure had been applied: whether or not the front sight "dipped" or "flipped" at the moment the hammer fell. This noting of sight movements (or movement of the entire gun) when the sixth shot is fired is the "Mayo Clinic" of shooting diagnosis. It is the alert that the shooter has faulty trigger-finger pressure: jerking, flinching, or heeling.

The shock of both the **whoom** of firing and the accompanying smack of recoil makes it impossible to distinguish sight (or gun) movements as the weapon is fired—the effect of noise and blast covers up any discernible movement. Therefore the shooter must count on the hammer falling on an empty chamber for the sixth shot to alert him to faulty trigger pressure, and to support his reading of the target.

Limited Area Scoring

Area practice is new, and it started by pure chance. A shipment of targets was delayed in arrival at Sacramento State College, and the available supply was exhausted in about the middle of the semester. However, there were plenty of 7-ring target centers on hand, and it was decided to use these small targets until the full targets arrived. At the time,

I remarked over the public address system for on-the-range lectures that shooting on 7-ring centers was going to penalize the jerkers, flinchers, and heelers, and each student should try to actuate the trigger with the correct trigger-finger motion as **no shots outside the 7-ring could be scored.**

I really felt sorry for the student-shooters who had not as yet learned the correct trigger pressure. In using the full target, a jerked, flinched, or heeled shot often hit in the 6-ring or in the 5-ring. Not too many of them were complete misses. In shooting on the 7-ring target centers, the struggling shooter lost these 5's and 6's and such hits were scored as big zeros. Scores in the 50's and 60's suddenly dropped to the 20's and 30's.

I began to feel a little better during the second week of using 7-ring target centers. The low-score shooters began to land their shots within the 7-rings. Apparently I had chanced on a means by which a shooter had the necessary motivation to overcome the desire to frame his shots and make the gun go off.

This limited area scoring is a stern discipline, but it is a device a shooter can use to force himself to overcome poor habits when pressing the trigger of a handgun.

Diagnosing Scores

A shooter must show improvement. Strangely, lack of improvement generally means a regression—lower and lower scores, poorer and poorer marksmanship. And it definitely means less enjoyment of shooting sessions.

Keeping track of average scores, the student-shooter has a fine opportunity for continual self-evaluation. Just as the precept of never firing a careless shot implies continual care in the digital dexterity of handgunning, so too will average scores afford a continual scanning of every shot fired. It is a matter of constant reading of the target and of watching the sights on the sixth shot in order to pinpoint faults for the corrective action that will improve shooting skills and provide the personal satisfaction of mastering handgun marksmanship.

Keep a record of all scores fired. Average weekly and monthly shooting scores. Make an analysis of these averages. Is the general trend upward or downward? What is the relationship of scores fired during slow fire without any time limit to scores fired under the pressure of a time limit? Scores and their trends over a week or more of shooting are symptomatic: good shooting procedures, high scores; poor procedures, low scores. A reading of each target fired will indicate a new or continuing fault requiring correction.

THE NINETY-DAY SHOOTING PROGRAM

Dry Shooting
Range Practice
Range Procedure
Rules of Conduct on the Range
First Sixty Days
Final Thirty-Day Period
Handgunning
Self-Diagnosis Tests

REALITY-TESTING OF PROGRAMMED PRACTICE IN HANDGUNNING INDI-cates that pistol and revolver shooting requires a three-month program of practice to develop basic skills. The first thirty days offer nothing more than an opportunity for a student-shooter to learn and to experiment with "nonlearning." The next month is a period of trial and error, of diagnosis and correction. The final thirty days are a polishing-up time, a period of systematic review of handgunning and its component parts: grip, position, sighting and aiming, and trigger pressure.

This ninety-day program in handgunning will teach a skill requiring muscular control as well as knowledge and understanding of theory. It is not enough that a shooter develop the muscular structure to hold the weight of a gun at arm's length without tension, nor merely gain the facts about shooting theory. It is vitally necessary that the student-shooter understand the reasons for the shooting theory outlined in this text, particularly the concepts of area aiming and the I-factors of trigger-finger motion. Any learning program must provide time to do things wrong and to make mistakes. It must also allow time for repetition of correct procedures. A ninety-day period is usually sufficient for most shooters.

There is a time lag to real development in learning any skill or sport while the learner tests reality. Coaches are aware of this fact—just as child psychologists know that reality-testing by youngsters is part of the learning process. Most good coaches in handgunning wait out their student-shooters, merely "marking time" until the shooter develops the combination of understanding and determination necessary for learning how to shoot a handgun with accuracy, speed, and safety. Good coaches do, however, utilize this time to develop muscles and pound away at basic concepts

of good shooting, and wait for M Day, the day that despera-
tion over continued inability to learn to shoot provides the
motivation to accept the shooting theory of area aiming and
a steadily increasing trigger pressure.

Possibly 10 percent of all beginning shooters can
learn to line up the sights, aim correctly, and shoot with the
proper trigger pressure. The remaining more average individuals ruin their aim by concentrating on the hold in relation to the bull's-eye, and become jerks, heelers, or flinchers.

A program for effective shooting, therefore, must con-
sider the difficulty the great majority of people have in over-
coming this psychological barrier. It must provide a drill in
the basic concepts at the same time it is providing for range
practice that will permit the shooter-student to reality-test his
own shortcuts to shooting skill. The program of instruction
must also put greater and greater demands upon the learning shooter to force a more rapid discovery of faults and
the need for corrective action. And it must build to the day
when skill is achieved: **the day the shooter learns to control
trigger pressure.**

Dry Shooting

Simulated firing—using the empty gun—has justly earned
the term of "dry shooting." It is difficult to maintain interest in any activity in which nothing happens. It is usually as uninteresting as any other routine exercise planned
to strengthen muscles. However, dry shooting can be interesting if it is planned as a drill in the basic techniques of
aiming and of trigger pressure. Interest can also be height-
ened if a definite schedule of practice is worked out for each
dry-shooting session and if this routine includes varied forms
of shooting: slow, time, and rapid-fire; both types of trigger

motion, single- and double-action; and both target and combat positions.

   If a routine of dry shooting is nothing more than
arm exercises, then only the muscular system is developed,
but if intelligent attempts are made to diagnose faults as
they occur in dry shooting, this practice can be invaluable.
It is in dry shooting that a shooter can learn to concentrate
actively on his sight alignment (intrasight relationship) while
learning to pace his trigger-finger motion at the subliminal
level. This is the conditioning process by which strict attention to sight alignment is keyed to a just-below-the-conscious
trigger-finger motion, but where the slightest fault in trigger
pressure intrudes instantly upon the concentration of the
shooter upon sight alignment.

   Dry shooting can be made to yield these dividends
when the student-shooter constantly searches for faulty procedures. Both grip and position are checked frequently, and
area aiming and the I-factors of trigger pressure are re-
viewed every time the handgun is aimed and the trigger is
actuated. Every shot in dry shooting can be a sixth shot for
the purpose of checking trigger-finger motion. Did the sights
or the gun move **as the hammer fell**? This is the question
possible on **every shot** in dry shooting. However, it must be
remembered that the "bait" to put sudden pressure on the
trigger does not exist in dry shooting. Shooters often find
trigger pressure when dry shooting no problem, but a severe
problem during range practice with a loaded gun.

Range Practice

On the pistol range the shooter has the opportunity to test
his skills, to put to trial the digital dexterity learned during
dry-shooting sessions. It is during sessions on the range that

the targets tell their story; and range shooting is the occasion for shooters to panic suddenly and to forget everything about area aiming and a steadily increasing trigger-finger motion.

There is a high interest potential in range practice, a reward when good shooting is achieved, and "punishment" when the attempt to shoot well fails. There are the constant effort to conduct an on-the-spot analysis of every

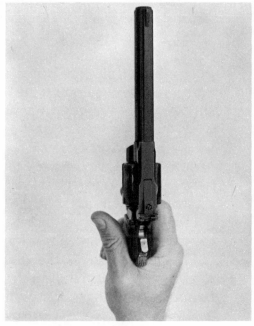

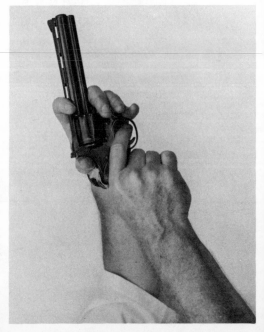

shot fired, the opportunity for experiencing the potential for disorganization when shooting live ammunition, and the occasion to check for the most common panic response: poor trigger pressure. In range firing there is the observable dip or flip of the front sight on the sixth shot; there are holes in a target for self-diagnosis or coaching by a fellow shooter.

Grip. Opposite top: Author demonstrates to a gunnery class at Sacramento State College the grip hazard of a "floating" thumb **(see close-up)** and instructs that the thumb must be against the frame of the handgun with a slight inward and downward pressure. **Opposite bottom:** Instruction on fitting the handgun into the hand for slow fire after the weapon is cocked. This methodology permits the shooter to have a full grip as he aims, except for a slight movement of the trigger finger. This is an advanced gunnery class and this technique is permissible only when 'the thumb of the nonshooting hand is inserted in front of the hammer **(see close-up)** to guard against any accidental discharge as the weapon is being fitted into the fingers of the shooting hand.

Tension-free positions. Note the level plane of the shoulders, the fully extended arm, the head position, and the lack of any strain in the neck area. Curtis Fuller is a student-coach at Sacramento State College and is demonstrating the correct position in a combat shooting class. The young lady is another student-coach and the author's daughter, Mary Ellen. She is demonstrating the correct position for a military weapon's session.

California combat sitting position. Student-coach Charles Lusbaugh demonstrates this well-structured position to a gunnery class at Sacramento State College.

Coaching. Gunnery classes at Sacramento State College use the student-coach method to enhance instruction. Students exchange roles, and all have an opportunity to view and correct another's mistakes. The coaches take a position immediately behind the shooter for safety control, communication, and observation **(left).** A particular task of the coach is to outline his student's handgun against a reference point (as in photo at right) and note if the weapon moves when the hammer falls on an empty chamber (sixth or eleventh shots, or when revolver specially loaded partly with empties to facilitate this observation). When the class moves downrange to examine targets **(below)**, the coach and student discuss possible faults as they view and paste the holes in each target. The author—at left center—supplements the student-coach's diagnosis of faults.

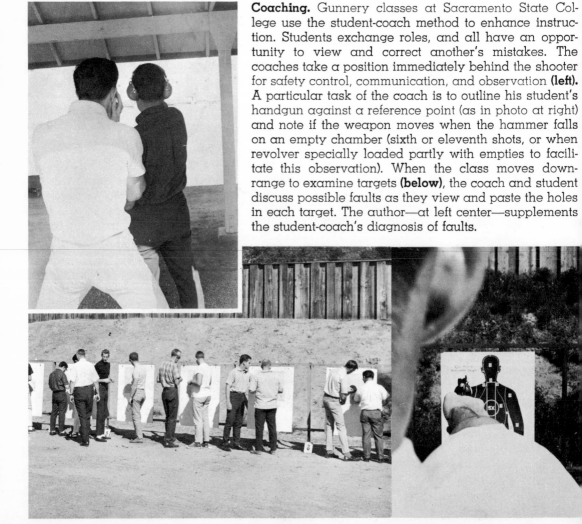

Coach and student. The team works together at all Sacramento State College classes. The coach's position is in support of the shooter and to further his tasks of observation and diagnosis of shooting faults. As these roles are reversed after each 10-shot relay of shooting, students benefit from this opportunity to view and correct the faults of a fellow student-shooter.

Handgun firing at Sacramento State College is often interspersed with group coaching sessions. The author **(at right)** reviews the two basic concepts of handgunning: area aiming and the I-factors of trigger motion.

Range Procedure

Visits to a shooting range will often involve shooting with a group under the guidance of a range officer. Therefore, some orientation to the range commands and expected conduct will help shooters to adapt to these surroundings. The commands and expected responses are as follows:

1. Five rounds, load. Come to the Raise Pistol position when ready. (Load five rounds and assume this position: muzzle down range, elbow bent, etc.)
2. Ready on the left. Ready on the right. (Sound off if **not** ready.)
3. All ready on the firing line. (No response; signifies three-second interval before next command.)
4. Commence firing. (May be verbal, whistle blast, or facing of targets toward shooter.)
5. Cease fire. (Stop shooting.)
6. Unload. (Empty weapon.)

When a range officer is ready to suspend firing to score and paste or replace targets, the commands are:

1. Make weapons safe. Cylinders out; slides back; guns on the bench.
2. Step back from firing line.
3. Advance and score.

Rules of Conduct on the Range

Accidents are **caused**, they do not **happen.** Range discipline **must be enforced.** Rules of conduct on handgun ranges are for the protection of everyone. Usually a range officer is designated for effective control. This might be any shooter but is usually an old hand. The basic rules for conduct on a range and the reasons for each rule are as follows:

1. **When back of the firing line, all unholstered guns must be unloaded, with cylinder out.**
   Reason: A gun with cylinder out cannot be accidentally discharged. When the cylinder is left open, the range officer, the shooter, and other participants in range shooting can always tell immediately whether the gun is loaded.
2. **Load only on command.**
   Reason: To ensure range control by range officer.
3. **Always keep gun muzzle down range.**
   Reason: In the event of any accidental discharge, bullet will go harmlessly into target area.
4. **No firing will be permitted until the command is given by the range officer.**
   Reason: To ensure range control so that shooters are not moving to or from the target, and the range is clear for firing.
5. **Fire only at assigned targets.**
   Reason: To ensure accurate scoring of each man's performance, and to keep the angle of fire at 90 degrees, thus lessening chances of ricochets.
6. **In case of misfires, hangfires, or "beep" shots, wait ten seconds, empty gun, check barrel for obstructions, and await orders.**
   Reason: A misfire or hangfire may delay firing for as much as seven seconds. If the revolver cylinder is rotated so that the chamber with the defective cartridge is no longer in line with the barrel, the gun will probably burst if the cartridge does fire. A "beep" shot occurs when a cartridge fires, but the gunpowder fails to ignite. The only noise of firing is the sound of the primer cap. Infrequently,

these faulty cartridges become hangfires; quite often, the energy of the primer cap is sufficient to move the bullet into but not out of the gun's barrel. The barrel must be visually checked for obstructions when a "beep" round is noted, occasionally only the primer will fire (usually caused by no powder in cartridge) but with enough force to push the bullet into the barrel though not enough force to push it through completely. A subsequent shot may cause the barrel to burst.

7. **Never talk to a shooter or distract his attention, unless you are his coach or the range officer.**
   Reason: You may cause him to swing the muzzle, endangering men on the line. This is especially true of novices who tend to be nervous.

8. **When firing is completed (or cease firing command is given) empty gun and lay it on the bench with its cylinder open. Never pick up a gun on the line while men are down range.**
   Reason: The range officer can immediately ascertain who has finished firing, and will know all weapons are harmless before he orders men forward to the targets to score.

9. **Never snap guns or dry fire in back of the firing line.**
   Reason: The opportunities for accidental discharge are minimized if guns are not closed. It is entirely possible that a man might forget to unload when leaving the firing line, or that a man might pick up another's gun which had been left loaded.

First Sixty Days

During this initial training period the shooter-student is expected to read all the preceding chapters of this text and to work hard at learning and understanding the basic concepts of handgunning. Dry-shooting practice should be on a 3 : 1 ratio with range practice: Three times the number of shots fired in range practice is the normal limit of a dry-shooting session during the same period. Don't dry shoot too much—unless dry shooting is checked against range firing to detect the possibility of newly acquired bad habits, it is' worthless.

The first four-week period of shooting builds up the slow-fire skills of the shooter and leads him into the time fire (five shots in twenty seconds) stage of pistol and revolver shooting. An outline for the first thirty days of planned shooting is as follows:

First Week. Slow fire, **two** targets (bull's-eye) at 25 yards of ten shots each for a total of twenty shots. **No more.** Concentrate on sight alignment and a steadily increasing trigger pressure. **Think about every shot fired.** This is the reason for the twenty-shot limitation. Shooting a great number of rounds leads to a blurring of the memory in regard to the poor shots. A sort of mental sugar-coating occurs. The student shoots and shoots, blasting out of his immediate recall all of the hits except those he wants to remember—the good shots. When dry shooting during this first week, try to recall the faults of range practice and attempt to achieve corrective action.

Second Week. Slow fire, **three** ten-shot targets (bull's-eye) at 25 yards for a total of thirty shots. Repeat, no more. Think about **every shot fired.** Read every target. Watch the sight and gun for movement on the sixth shot. Work during dry-shooting sessions to correct faults discovered during the last range session. If shooting a revolver single action be careful not to "thumb" it, to let the hammer slip from under your thumb. In cocking the gun keep the sights as close to alignment as possible—do not wave the muzzle in circles. At this time it is also well to practice "lowering the hammer" —for instances when a revolver is cocked in single action and it is decided not to fire it. Use care, let the hammer down halfway, then take your finger off the trigger and lower the hammer with your thumb. Shoot twice this week on the pistol range, if possible.

Third Week. Thirty shots slow fire at 25 yards and ten rounds time fire on the bull's-eye target for a total of forty rounds. Work at self-diagnosis and correction. Seek cadence in time fire. Try to relate the trigger-finger motion in time fire to the pacing of trigger pressure generally. Two range sessions in this week are desirable.

Fourth Week. Ten rounds of "first shot" practice on a bull's-eye target at 25 yards. This is slow fire in which the arm is extended for every shot and returned to the "Raise Pistol" position between shots. Trigger-finger motion is paced as in the initial shot of a time or rapid-fire string. The shot is not hurried, nor is it timed, but no time can be lost. Remember that the remaining four shots of each five-shot string must be fired in the time left after the first shot is fired. Round out each range session with a repeat of the third week's program, shooting a total of forty additional shots, firing thirty in slow fire and ten in time fire. One to three sessions on the pistol range in this week are desirable.

Fifth Week. Work on known faults. Allow up to thirty rounds of ammunition for corrective practice on the pistol range during each practice session. Use a blank target (no bull's-eye) or the new area aiming target (a 7-inch square outlined in black) in order to fight against the habit of framing the shot. If there is no bull's-eye as a reference point, it is possible to forget it and concentrate on sight alignment and trigger pressure. In this blank target practice, be certain not to look **through** the sights, and be sure to let the gun swing naturally within the aiming area in which you can hold the gun. Possibly another check-up device may be useful. This is "Swiss-loading," and it is used mainly with revolvers. Ask a fellow shooter to pick up a few live rounds and a few empties, mix them up, and load the revolver's chambers, then spin the cylinder and close it. You will not know which chambers hold the live cartridges. Now, aim and fire the gun in a normal manner, but **watch the sights for movement as the hammer falls.** This is the same procedure as the "alert" of the sixth shot, but it provides a greater number of instances in which the hammer falls without actually firing a cartridge. Remember, the blast and kick of shooting cover up faults in trigger-finger motion. It is only when the hammer falls, but does not fire a cartridge, that sight movement will alert a shooter to **sudden** trigger pressure, and the reactions of flinching and heeling as well. Finish up each session this week with twenty rounds of slow fire and twenty rounds of time fire on the bull's-eye target at 25 yards. In dry-shooting sessions concentrate on pacing the trigger motion for rapid fire, learning to align the sights quickly and recover the aim as fast as possible. Try to shoot two or three times on the pistol range during this fifth week.

　　Sixth and Seventh Weeks. Continue the self-diagnosis and remedial action, allowing 50 percent of the ammunition expended during each range session for corrective practice. Work hard at correcting errors. At the close of each session shoot ten rounds of slow, time, and rapid fire on a bull's-eye target at 25 yards. One or two lengthy sessions a week is sufficient at this time. Rest and think—reflect on past shooting sessions.

　　Eighth Week. Range practice during the eighth week can be limited to one shooting session. This should be a testing session in which the shooter fires the "Camp Perry" target (9 and 10 in the black) at 25 yards for a total of thirty shots: ten shots in slow, in time, and in rapid fire. Time allowances are twenty seconds in time fire for each string of five shots, and ten seconds for each five shots in rapid fire. Fire "the course" (thirty shots slow, time, and rapid) once, and then fire thirty rounds at whichever stage requires more practice.

When satisfied, refire the course. This is the start of your "average." No one can say just what any individual should shoot at this stage of his program, for there are too many individual physical and emotional variables involved, but it is safe to state that from this point the average score must be improved—or the shooter is disregarding opportunity after opportunity to find his faults and to correct them.

Final Thirty-Day Period

Shoot as often as possible during these last four weeks of the ninety-day program, but do not allow a week to go by without shooting on the range at least once. Range practice and dry-shooting sessions—plus exercises with a weight and a hand grip or small rubber ball—will place a shooter in condition to fire from ninety to a hundred rounds in each range session during this last month of programmed instruction. No one can learn to shoot unless a considerable amount of ammunition is expended during this period. Later, after basic skills are attained, it is not necessary to shoot as often to maintain the learned-skill level, but this is still the learning period, and practice, practice, and practice are required.

The intelligent shooter is the individual who utilizes exercise and dry shooting—and his "extra" firing on the range—to work out some shooting difficulty. This is usually trigger-finger motion, a popular fault. Some shooters continue to look **through** the sights at the target, rather than utilizing the intrarelationship of the two sights **within** the sight radius, but this is not common during the last month of a shooting program that stresses testing and diagnosis.

As each range session concludes, determine an average score each time the course is fired (thirty rounds: slow,

An "A" grade in the final examination.

time, and rapid) and compare it with the previous week's average, and with the overall average to date. Study each ten-shot total at each stage of the course. Is the fault in the slow-fire stage? In time fire? During rapid fire? Remember, each stage of fire complements the others. Forget the classic alibi that any particular type of fire is difficult or impossible to learn. If you can shoot slow fire, then you can shoot at a more rapid rate. In fact, the more rapid types of shooting often teach a better trigger-finger motion for slow fire. During the final week concentrate on the type of shooting that is poorest—and improve your skill. In fact, this will become standard procedure—seek to improve areas of weakness, and total skill will be achieved.

Handgunning

Handgunning is one of the most rewarding sports today. No matter what the skill level of the shooter or how often a handgun is fired, there is a test situation. The target—on the range, in the hunting field, or in combat—is both a confrontation and a challenge. The paper target on the range returns a blank stare to the shooter, saying in effect, "Let's see how good you are," and then displays the shooter's response visually. The charging animal or the armed opponent states the same proposition—but the shooter may be in the hospital or the morgue if the challenge is not met and overcome.

It costs money to learn to shoot, but it is not really expensive. A .22-caliber handgun cuts the cost of practice. Modern reloading machines are available at low cost for the big-bore shooters, and this hobby further reduces the expense of shooting. It is money well spent, however, to buy both recreational and protective skills.

Join a good club, one with range facilities. Shoot with others. Write the National Rifle Association if your locality does not have a club and range; they supply data on where to shoot and how to form a club. Seek help in your local sporting goods store, for most owners and employees in these shops know of a place to shoot and of other persons with similar interests. Most police departments will also cooperate. Seek out the members of the department who like shooting (not clerical personnel), talk to them, and seek their aid and advice—and possibly permission to use the police range.

Lastly, find a fellow shooter as a partner. Shoot a coach-and-pupil session or two with him, discussing the concepts in this text. Go to the range as a team. Try to help each other, but also shoot **against** each other. This is the challenge of any game. Try to win—to shoot better than your chosen partner. Indulge in some bull sessions devoted to postmortems of the range practice. Discuss exercises and dry shooting. Many shooters split the cost of a reloading device with their shooting partner. This not only makes the reloading hobby more interesting, but also provides a further opportunity for discussion of shooting faults and remedial action. One or both of you may decide to join the National Rifle Association (**The American Rifleman** is worth the cost of dues). This is the official organization for all of us who enjoy shooting as a sport and recreation as well as for individuals who carry handguns as a condition of employment in a law enforcement agency.

The skills of handgunning must be learned, but it is one of the few sports that provides an extra dividend: It may someday save your life.

POPULAR "LITTLE" HANDGUN

The Smith & Wesson 5-shot **Chief's Special** fires the .38 S & W Special cartridge, but measures only 6½ inches overall with its 2-inch barrel and scales a mere 19 ounces. It is a favorite of off-duty police officers. In a "speed" holster it is an excellent personal defense weapon.

The Best in American Autopistols. Above: Smith & Wesson 9mm double-action autopistol. **Below:** The Colt .45 Gold Cup National Match. Both pistols are chambered for cartridges with excellent stopping characteristics and they are fine personal defense guns.

Top American Revolvers. Above: the ventilated-rib Colt Python. **Below:**
The heavy-frame Smith & Wesson Magnum. Both guns are chambered
for the .357 Magnum, excellent for hunting and defense; both guns will
also shoot the shorter and less powerful .38 Special cartridge, a favorite of
hand-loaders for target shooting.

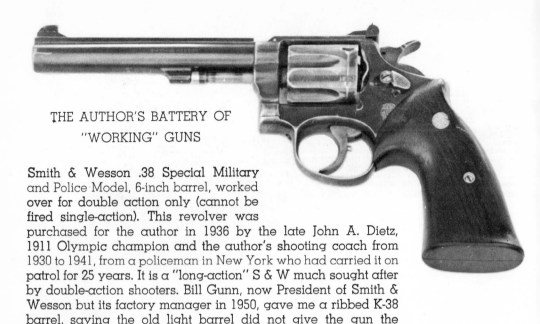

THE AUTHOR'S BATTERY OF "WORKING" GUNS

Smith & Wesson .38 Special Military and Police Model, 6-inch barrel, worked over for double action only (cannot be fired single-action). This revolver was purchased for the author in 1936 by the late John A. Dietz, 1911 Olympic champion and the author's shooting coach from 1930 to 1941, from a policeman in New York who had carried it on patrol for 25 years. It is a "long-action" S & W much sought after by double-action shooters. Bill Gunn, now President of Smith & Wesson but its factory manager in 1950, gave me a ribbed K-38 barrel, saying the old light barrel did not give the gun the muzzle-heaviness he believed necessary and designed into the K-38 series, and recently he contributed a **U**-shaped main spring of his own design. Steve Herrett, the pistol-stock customizer, recently carved out the grips to match the overall dimensions of my other working revolvers in the Colt Python series. The small external trigger stop in the rear of the trigger was installed by the late Bob Pardua of New York's police ballistic squad. A remarkable gun that can still deliver 2½- to 3-inch groups at 25 yards from the standard offhand position. George Hyde, Brooklyn's only gunsmith whose mechanical know-how was obtained during many years with Germany's Mauser complex, examined it in 1957 and said the original case-hardened hammer and trigger and other internal parts had not been worn by continual use over many years but had **only been polished.**

Colt's .45 Gold Cup. This is a recent acquisition, after retiring a beat-up Government Model that continued to shoot over the years only because of a George Hyde "accuracy" job in the forties and a Bob Chow tune-up in the fifties. Hyde was the top gunsmith around New York; Bob Chow is the premier mechanic in the West. The new Gold Cup is a fabulous gun with its own built-in "accuracy" tune-up. The first few Sundays of shooting turned in all-in-the-black groups at 25 yards on the Standard American target, ranging about 4 to 5 inches average size.

Opposite: Colt .357 Python purchased in 1967 from a police science student in the author's gunnery class at Sacramento State College. During the summer of 1967 it was fired 9,000 times with full-charge police ammunition in tests of the work of the gunsmithing class at Lassen Junior College in Susanville, California, in alternate installations of 2-, 4-, and 6-inch barrels. During the winter of 1967–1968, a total of 12,000 rounds was fired from the offhand position in slow, time, and rapid fire, again with the interchange of different barrels, in a test for **Guns and Hunting** magazine to determine "hand-held" accuracy (the use of the same gun with different length barrels removed many variables concerned with trigger pressure and lock time from this research). It was then shot in 2½" barrel tests of accuracy and functioning with alternating .357 magnum and .38 Special full-charge police cartridges for a total of above 5,000 rounds. Joe Gannon of Colt Firearms processed the gun mechanically after all this shooting and interchange of barrels, reported it as good as new, and installed a new 6-inch barrel with a brood front sight. Since that time it has been fired weekly by the author as a single-action target revolver, an average of 600 shots a week.

Smith & Wesson's .22-caliber automatic pistol. A gift from the late Carl R. Hellstrom, when he was president of this firm. It was one of their first run and has been fired over 25,000 rounds without a malfunction of any kind. The muzzle brake is weird-looking, but serves to hold the gun down in rapid fire. The grips are by "Fitz" with an adjustable bottom handrest that compensates for the muzzle-heaviness of this weapon. An accurate gun and a pleasant weapon to shoot.

Ruger's .22 automatic pistol. Another recent acquisition for the purpose of testing an "economy" weapon in this popular caliber and model. To date it has performed excellently, without malfunction and with accuracy.

Self-diagnosis Tests

An understanding of the two basic concepts of modern hand-gunning concerned with aiming and trigger motion is a prerequisite to accurate shooting. Area aiming and the I-factors in trigger-finger motion are the key areas upon which self-diagnosis should be concentrated. Answer the following questions selected from the final examination of Sacramento State College's gunnery course. Compare responses with the key answers listed after the tests, and review subject areas in which questions were answered incorrectly. A full understanding of all the facets of both of these basic concepts in handgunning, aiming, and trigger motion, requires a correct answer to all the questions on these two tests.

Test No. 1—Area Aiming

1. The most important factor in sighting and aiming is:
   a. The front sight.
   b. The rear sight.
   c. The interrelationship of both sights.
   d. The arc between the sights and the target.
2. A "line of sight" is established by:
   a. Aligning the two sights with each other.
   b. Looking at the target, after assuming the correct position.
   c. Looking at the sights, after assuming the correct position.
   d. By "shuttling" the eyes between the two aligned sights and the target.
3. In sighting and aiming a handgun, the most important

relationship is:

a. The alignment of front and rear sights with each other.

b. The alignment of sights on the target.

c. A clearly defined front sight.

4. The basic principle of area aiming is:

a. So long as the weapon is aimed somewhere in the shooter's normal aiming area it is correct to squeeze the shot off.

b. It is impossible to hold the pistol absolutely steady. Therefore, when the beginning shooter sees the bull's-eye clearly, even momentarily, he should squeeze the trigger.

c. Attempting to hold the pistol as steady as possible at the six o'clock hold.

d. To "hold" in an area that is centered on the bull's-eye.

5. Area aiming is a concept based upon the fact that most shooters do better when they settle for "half a loaf," rather than attempting the physically unattainable. True_____ False_____

6. The proper area for the beginning shooter to hold in for area aiming is an area equal to the 7-ring on a bull's-eye pistol target. True_____ False_____

7. The sight alignment should be the same for every shot. True_____ False_____

8. A shooter's eyes can be focused on the sights of a handgun and on the target 25 yards distant at the same time. True_____ False_____

9. In getting the correct sight alignment, the front sight is more important than the rear sight. True_____ False_____

10. Fuzzy, blurry, or hairy sights indicate the shooter is looking:

a. At his sights.

b. Through his sights.

c. Through only one eye.

d. At the sights with both eyes closed.

Test No. 2—Trigger Motion

1. "Squeeze the grip" is a clue to effective trigger-finger motion. True_____ False_____
2. Coaches and shooters may be alerted to an incorrect trigger motion by watching the "happening" when the "sixth" shot is "fired"—the hammer unexpectedly falls on an empty chamber. True_____ False_____
3. There is insufficient time to squeeze the trigger properly in timed and rapid fire. True_____ False_____
4. "Calling the shot" means telling the instructor where you believe your last shot hit the target.
   True_____ False_____
5. When a marksman makes his revolver "go off" when it is on his point of aim for a moment, or when its swing-and-sway diminishes momentarily, he will find his shots hitting the target:
   a. Away from where his revolver was aimed when fired.
   b. Quite close to where the revolver was aimed when fired.
   c. Low and left.
6. In pistol shooting, most poor scores result from the attempt to be:
   a. Too precise in aiming.
   b. A fast shooter.
   c. Too careful of trigger-finger motion.
7. When the shooter jerks the trigger the point of impact is usually directly beneath the bull's-eye, at six o'clock.
   True_____ False_____
8. "Calling the shot" means telling the instructor if you are firing slow fire, timed fire, or rapid fire.
   True_____ False_____
9. "Heeling" the gun means that it is likely the point of impact will be in what is known as the "12 to three o'clock area." True_____ False_____
10. The desire to excel and be too precise in sighting and

aiming is the psychological basis for trigger jerking.
True_____ False_____

11. When the sights move abruptly when the hammer falls on an empty chamber or a fired cartridge, it is an indication of:
   a. Nervousness.
   b. Lack of practice or holding weight out at the end of the shooting arm.
   c. Jerking the trigger.
   d. Correct trigger-finger motion.

12. "Freezing on the trigger" is related to the characteristic of trigger motion described as:
   a. Cadence.
   b. Increasing.
   c. Imperceptible.
   d. None of the foregoing.

13. The desire to excel and be too precise in sighting and aiming is the psychological basis for:
   a. Good pistol shooting.
   b. "Framing" a shot.
   c. Effective sight alignment.
   d. Area aiming.

14. The point of impact when the shooter jerks the trigger with a sudden pressure and does not, in addition, "flinch" or "heel" the weapon is usually:
   a. Above the bull's-eye.
   b. Below the bull's-eye.
   c. Below the bull's-eye and to the left.
   d. Above the bull's-eye and to the right.

15. Trigger motion should be:
   a. Very rapid.
   b. Straight to the rear.
   c. Stop and go.
   d. Very, very slow.

16. Which of the following is the best description of effective

trigger pressure?
a. Increasing trigger-finger motion, straight to the rear.
b. Independent and imperceptible trigger-finger motion.
c. Imperceptible, independent, increasing trigger-finger motion.
d. Independent, steadily increasing trigger-finger motion straight to the rear.

17. Trigger-finger pressure upon the trigger is increased:
a. As an equal pressure is exerted upon the grip by the remaining fingers of the gun hand.
b. Steadily.
c. As the weapon steadies upon its "holding" point.
d. Suddenly.

18. The tendency to "make" a handgun "go off" usually results because a student shooter:
a. Is afraid of the recoil and the weapon.
b. Does not know any better.
c. Has a normal desire to excel, and "frames" a shot, attempting to be too precise in sighting and aiming.
d. Is unable to hold the weapon steady.

19. The most graphic device to prove to a shooter that he is "jerking" the trigger is:
a. To use "Swiss" or "staggered" chamber loading—five cartridges mixed with fired cases.
b. To point out the characteristic impact area on the target.
c. To permit the marksman to shoot at a blank target.
d. To explain psychological causation.

20. "Flinching" and "heeling" result from knowing the weapon is about to go off (jerking the trigger) and:
a. Anticipation of recoil.
b. Anticipation of trigger slap.
c. Anticipation of gun "dipping."
d. Anticipation of sight alignment moving away from aiming point.

Answers Test No. 1—Area Aiming

1. C
2. B
3. A
4. A
5. True
6. True
7. True
8. False
9. False
10. B

Answers Test No. 2—Trigger Motion

1. False
2. True
3. False
4. True
5. A
6. A
7. False
8. False
9. True
10. True
11. C
12. B
13. B
14. C
15. B
16. C
17. B
18. C
19. A
20. A

INDEX

A

Aiming, area, 45–60
  away theory, 47, 60
  calling shots, 58–60, 100–1
  concept of, 47–52
  framing shots, 56–57
  hold, 57
  muscle building for, 52–55
  nerve control for, 56–57
  size of area, 51
  stagger or "Swiss" loading, 49
  target, 54, 98
  test, 129–31, 134
American Rifleman, 123
Autopistol, 5

B

Backslap, trigger, 71–72

C

Cadence, *see* Trigger-finger motion
California sitting position, 29, 112
Calling shots, 58–60, 100–1
Coaching, 112–13
Combat shooting
  double-action, 27–30, 112
  grip, 79–81
  hip-shooting, 83–93
  "milking" the trigger, 81–82
  positions, 27–30, 112
Corrective action, faults, 95–104
  coaching, 112–13
  diagnosing scores, 103–4

  targets, 97–98
  dry shooting, 108–9
  gun movement, 6th shot, 101–2
  limited area scoring, 102–3
  miscalled shots, 100–1
  practice shooting program,
    116–22
  tests, self-diagnosis, 129–34
Creep, trigger, 71

D

Diagnosis of faults, *see* Corrective
  action
Directed fire, 83–93
Double-action shooting, 76–82
  "bumping" trigger motion, 92–93
  grip, 79–81
  "milking" the trigger, 81–82,
    92–93
  rapid cadence in hip shooting,
    92–93
  straight-through trigger pressure,
    78–79
  two-stage trigger motion, 77–78

E

Ear protection, 54
Examinations, 129–34
Eyes, *see* Vision

F

Faults, *see* Corrective action